EARLY STUFF

EARLY STUFF
Copyright © 2013 & 2020 by Sam Pink

Cover art copyright © 2020 by Sam Pink

Cover design by Tyler Crumrine

Edited by Cameron Pierce

Paperback ISBN: 978-1-948687-16-4
Hardcover ISBN: 978-1-948687-17-1
ebook ISBN (EPUB): 978-1-948687-18-8

LCCN: 2019956147

This book may not be reproduced in whole or in part, except for the inclusion of brief quotations in a review, without permission in writing from the author or publisher. No part of this publication may be reproduced, stored in or introduced into retrieval system, or transmitted, in any form, or by any means (electronic, mechanical, photocopying, recording, or otherwise), without prior permission of the publisher.

Requests for permission should be directed to 1111@1111press.com, or mailed to 11:11 Press LLC, 4757 15th Ave S., Minneapolis, MN 55407.

FIRST EDITION
9 8 7 6 5 4 3 2 1

EARLY STUFF

SAM PINK

you are walking past
a cemetery, and you
think, "oh yeah, that's right."

TABLE OF CONTENTS

001
SELECTIONS FROM
I AM GOING TO CLONE MYSELF THEN KILL
THE CLONE AND EAT IT

085
FROWNS NEED FRIENDS TOO

261
NO ONE CAN DO ANYTHING WORSE TO YOU
THAN YOU CAN

397
GERALD MCCLELLAN VERSUS NIGEL BENN

SELECTIONS FROM I AM GOING TO CLONE MYSELF THEN KILL THE CLONE AND EAT IT

TODAY I HOPE A BUS ACCIDENTALLY KILLS ME

Today I hope a bus accidentally kills me. That way, people will look back on everything I did in my life and think about how special it was, because a bus accidentally killed me. The driver wouldn't have to feel bad, because it'd be an accident. And if for some reason the collision didn't kill me, when the driver got out of the bus to check on me, I'd say, "Could you please roll over my head and finish me. I'm in pain and I want to become a hero." People nearby would see the big wheel of the bus smashing my skull into the concrete—my screaming mouth the last thing to go.

I AM THE BEST THING EVER INTRODUCED TO THE MATERIAL WORLD

Sometimes I don't eat dinner because I'm worried someone will kill me if I leave my room.

I wish there was a cord attached to my forehead that I could pull to raze my skull like one of those collapsible puppets.

When I get home tonight I will close my eyes in the doorway and walk to my room with my eyes closed and go to bed and keep my eyes closed until I fall asleep.

If I swallowed your eye you'd see a big pile of undigested leaves, and the leaves would be covered in caterpillars.

If I were immortal I would go to outerspace and float forever.

Earth and space are the daydream of very tired people.

But you know what, I'm awesome.

And I am glad to meet you.

You will be my friend until I say something to you in person that frightens you.

And I don't know anything about anyone but myself, and even that is uninteresting.

My goal is to interfere with other people as little as possible and be gone from earth without a sound.

ABSOLUTE HUMAN ABOLITION

On the way to the mailbox today, I slipped on some ice and almost hit my eye on a tree branch. Then I regained my balance and continued on. The guy walking behind me laughed. He had every right to laugh because it was funny and he had no tie to the physical pain I could've experienced. However, if I had lost my eye, I would've walked up to him and held him down in the snow—and let the blood from my empty eye socket spill into his laughing mouth. My mail was mostly things about credit cards and coupons I will never use.

SHORT PLAY

A pizza delivery person stands at the front door of someone's house. He goes to knock again but then hears someone undoing the lock. A man opens the door.

PIZZA DELIVERY PERSON: Here you are sir. It's fourteen eighty five.

MAN: [taking the pizza] Uh, ok. Hold on [reaches for his wallet] Uh, do you want to come in? You can come in if you want. I'll give you some of my pizza here and we can watch tv or something—whatever you like to do. I have board games.

PIZZA DELIVERY PERSON: [stops chewing gum and squints at the man] What?

MAN: Yeah. Come on in.

[The pizza delivery guys pops a bubble. Then he is quiet.]

MAN: [softly] Please. Please stay. We can talk or I can make you laugh maybe. Come on–please? I'll pay you for the pizza but please stay.

PIZZA DELIVERY PERSON: No thanks sir. That's fourteen eighty five, please.

MAN: [clears his throat] Isn't there anything I can do to get you to please please please stay even for ten minutes. It's so bad in there.

PIZZA DELIVERY PERSON: There is nothing you can do to get me to stay. Please pay sir. [then slowly] There is nothing you can do to get me to stay—nothing.

MAN: [looks at the pizza box] That's what I thought.

MOVE IN WITH ME

Move in with me. I'm lonely. We can watch television together. We'll laugh at people who make funny observations. When you get hungry, I'll make you food. You'll say, "Man, I could go for…" and I'll make it. I'll put little pieces of glass in the food. Your mouth will flood with blood. You'll tell me something that happened to you during the day and every word will sound pathetic coming through your swollen and cut lips and tongue. I'll say, "Don't talk with your mouth full, it makes you look impolite." You'll put your head in my lap after we eat and I'll put my hands over your face and touch it. My hands will feel heavy on your face. You'll get really uncomfortable and ask to take a shower to clean the feeling off. We'll take a shower together and I'll pinch your ass. You'll laugh. I'll let myself slip to the floor of the shower. The water will roam your back and slip from your ass and hit me in the face. I'll drink the water before it enters the drain. There will be a lot of hair clogging the drain. I'll take it out and put it on my lips like a goatee and I'll act like a middle-aged man who has a goatee. I'll wear sandals and a shirt that says the name of a town in Mexico. I'll kiss you on the lips with my goatee. When you leave the shower, you'll turn the faucet to cold and my heart will hiccup. I'll feel afraid. I'll follow you into my room. While you're toweling off, I'll lock the door and say, "Pray to your god, it's time to suffer. I want to make you level-eyed with my nightmare." Then I'll pause before saying, "Just kidding." I'll jump on the bed naked. You'll say, "Your balls look funny." I'll say, "Like 'Family Circus' funny or what?" Then we'll have sex. When we're done, I'll clean myself off with some tissue paper and the tissue paper will stick to me.

I'll hop around the room like a white-tailed deer. You'll put on an orange coat and paint your face with camouflage. You'll say, "Come here little deer, I won't hurt you." Then you'll shoot me in the neck and there will be a huge hole in my neck and the blood will leak into my throat. And we'll sit back down, because between every action there is quiet. "Paint my toes," you'll eventually say, your voice sounding way too loud against the quiet. I'll hold your feet in my hands and paint your toes. I'll feel like crushing the bones. I'll say, "You have nice feet, would you mind if I crushed them with a hammer or a dumbbell." You'll laugh and ask me to turn off the lights so we can sleep. I'll turn off the lights and lie down next to you. You'll fall asleep faster than me and it will rain. The rain will beat the window. I'll open the window and hold out a glass. When the glass is full, I'll drink it. I'll put on some of your lipstick and spit all over my groin. I'll kiss the wall and punch the lipstick stain. I'll feel like obliterating myself. I'll feel like going outside and drowning in a puddle. Just lying down and resting. I'll put some old leaves underneath my eyelids. And the weight of the sky will crush me into rest. I'll wish for this in painful quiet. In painful quiet I'll wish for you to wake up so I won't be alone. But you'll sleep and I'll wait, hoping to be relieved—if only for a second—of the mounting weight that wipes its feet at my door every night.

MANNEQUINS THAT SWEAT BLACK INK AND NEVER HAVE ANY FUN

I hunt bugs with a miniature bow made of twigs, and arrows fashioned from the creases in your face that represent every time you have frowned.

I am in a retirement home and I am sleeping underneath the bed of an old man who doesn't know who he is anymore and who thinks his family has disappeared. And I keep saying, "Tick tock tick tock, nobody loves you and I won't hold your hand when you die."

If you put red licorice in your ear it looks like your ear is vomiting blood.

If I ever have kids it will be a mistake. And I will apologize to the largest number of people willing to listen.

I wish I were the person you imagine yourself to be because then you'd love me and never let me go.

Lie down; it's time for me to walk over you and call you a bridge I no longer need.

I love everyone who reads this.

AN INCOMPLETE LIST OF THE THINGS I'D LIKE TO BE REINCARNATED AS

A band-aid with a little bit of blood on it and the blood has become brown from being old.

An old man who never dies.

The wind that dried the words in your mouth before you said them—when we were on a walk and thinking about hating each other.

A kite stuck in a tree at six p.m. on an October afternoon with enough wind necessary to constantly push the kite against the tree but not free it.

The blood trapped in your muscles when they clench during an orgasm.

The heat in your mouth.

A body of water filled with skeletons floating like ice cubes— and only the first few feet below the surface allows any sun so the rest is a color no one's ever seen.

An eyelash of yours that falls to the sidewalk then blows into a discarded aluminum can.

A dog that doesn't worry about anything and just eats garbage all day (and also maybe fucks some other homeless dogs too because eating garbage would suck).

The very end of all your laughs.

The fold of skin that collects the most dirt on your body.

A large hill upon which someone you love loses their breath and dies—facedown in the grass.

Myself, because I'll never be done.

APARTMENT

Every time I come home I stand in the doorway and say,
"It's time for a monster to eat me now."

Then it does.

When I go to bed and pull the covers open I say,
"It's time for a monster to eat me now."

Then it does.

Every time I get out of bed I say,
"It's time for a monster to eat me now."

Then it does.

Every time I leave my apartment I say,
"It's time for a monster to eat me now."

Then it does.

ROLLER HOCKEY

When I was ten I used to play roller hockey with the kid who lived across the street. One time his dad came out while we were playing and he got in goal. He said he used to play hockey and that we didn't know what we were doing. Then he asked me to get my dad "out 'ere, and see ifee can man-up." I told him my dad was at work. Then he tried to show me how to hold my stick the right way. His breath smelled like whiskey. He kept pushing me. He said, "That's what hockey is about." Five minutes later, his son and I decided we didn't want to play hockey anymore and that we'd rather swim in the pool in his backyard. As we walked to the pool, the dad said, "Hey, don't be pissin in my pool. Arright? I wouldn't swim in your toilet so don't be pissin in my pool." Later on, while pissing in his pool, I thought to myself, "I wouldn't mind if he swam in my toilet because then it would be easy for me to shit on him. Real easy."

I ENVY THE MOON BECAUSE IT NEVER HAS TO FACE THE DAY

When I put my ear against your stomach, I hear a storm.

When I put my eyelashes by your tongue and blink real fast, you get a horrified look on your face and I say, "There is a spider tap-dancing on your tongue and I hope you are comfortable because right now will never be over."

And if you pray with your eyes closed real tight, god will make sure no one cuts your legs off.

I lie on the floor and roll over everything that I encounter and when I encounter something I can't roll over, I sleep next to it and hold its eyes shut until it thinks it has died.

Each new relationship is made of cotton and I am a bee that is on fire, lost and ready to land.

And my head is a broken toy.

I hate my head.

And if you don't hate yourself, no one will.

And your broken skull is not a puzzle, it's just garbage.

So be ugly for me or I will hammer a nail into your ear.

You're pathetic and I draw the world on your face before I

step on it.

I put the shit that comes out of your mouth beneath your nose.

I sit in my room and cut circles out of the dark and throw them beneath you, hoping hoping hoping hoping hoping that you will fall somewhere I don't even know about, somewhere I couldn't even reach my hand into if I wanted.

Because you are afraid to die.

Because you haven't begun to make it necessary yet.

Because your whole life is a fucking coloring book.

Please change your mind.

I was here first.

MOST PEOPLE ARE NOT AS GOOD AS ME

A sunburned homeless man came up to me yesterday and showed me his forearm. There was a gaping wound along the bone, barely held together by office staples. The wound leaked clear liquid. I gave him what was in my pockets—70 cents. That was probably enough to buy more staples. Enough to keep his wound somewhat cured. And me? I'm so great it hurts.

HELP ME

I would like to cut off the fingers from my right hand and replace them with all pinky fingers. I would wave the fingers and my hand would look like an underwater plant. I am willing to pay up to five hundred dollars to have this done by a relatively competent doctor or finger expert or even someone who knows what an underwater plant looks like, so they could be like, "Yes" or "No, that doesn't look like an underwater plant."

IF YOU WERE MY BLOOD
I'D OVERDOSE ON HEROIN

I'm sorry.

I didn't want to be at your place when my head broke into pieces all over the floor, spreading out over your tile.

And I didn't want for you to have to watch me clean it up—slowly—big pieces first, then the smaller ones.

I'm sorry.

But if you look at things a certain way, you are always on top of the Earth's curve. And someone is saying "ta-da" wherever you go, but no one is clapping. And that's good because clapping is the sound of things going wrong.

I'm going to smash your arms and legs and pour the dust into an hourglass and measure how long it takes me to forget that I'm one of billions of people who showed up to the party uninvited and with nothing in their hands.

I'm sorry.

VOLUNTARY DEATH

At the post office I saw an old man sitting in his wheelchair. His face was a very slow waterfall. A little girl walked up to him and tugged on his sleeve and asked him a question. As he answered, he drooled into his lap. He drooled a long glassy cord. Then he wiped his mouth with an American flag handkerchief tucked underneath the collar of his shirt. The little girl said, "Ewww" and walked away.

SELFISH ASSHOLE

You're mean. You didn't leave your window unlocked last night. You didn't leave your window unlocked and I couldn't come into your house. I couldn't give you kisses while you were sleeping. And I couldn't sit in your dark room and feel like the darkness was dyeing my skin. I couldn't pull the blanket over your exposed leg, and pat the blanket down and say, "There you go." And I couldn't take a shower and use your apricot-cucumber soap and see my pubes stick to the bar. I couldn't put my mouth over your cat's head and just stand there while it scratched my face. And I couldn't put little bombs in between your teeth. I couldn't split you down the middle with a box cutter and get inside and hang a picture that says, "Home is inside the person you kind of hate and have sliced open with a box cutter." And I couldn't clip my fingernails and secrete the clippings somewhere behind your couch in the hopes that another me would grow and relieve me of my responsibility to you. I couldn't pick off a scab and put it in your strawberry jelly (because if there's one person I want to eat my scabs, it's you baby, it's you). And I couldn't sit by your bed and shove a flower into your ear so you'd finally look pretty. I couldn't lift your leg and put my head beneath and constantly drop your leg so it looks like you're kicking me. And I couldn't lift your arm and see your armpit hair grow. I couldn't push my face into your armpit hair and pretend like I was at a carwash. And I definitely couldn't make some tea and then throw it at your sleeping face and say, "Here's some tea, just how you like it." I couldn't ultimately decide that I wanted to run back outside. And I couldn't climb back out the window and look for another window. Because someone is always going to leave their window open for me.

PUBIC HAIR THAT IS HARD WITH BLOOD

I would like to blow up my left eye with a small firecracker.

I would like the firecracker to be large enough to totally explode my eye, but small enough to leave the rest of my head intact (maybe just blacken the socket a little).

I am the process of billions of years of motion and the predecessor of billions more.

And the grass along the sidewalk in front of my apartment is green during the day and black at night and I am always the same.

Look at the dirt on my face and I will look at the dirt on your face and we will never stop having a very painful orgasm.

I would like to camp out in one of your pores. And set up a scaffold on your face and keep it clean. You wouldn't have to pay me anything. I would wash your face with my tongue and hopefully a small mop of some sort (or ideally, a small mop made of tongues).

I would also like to rub my face against the carpet until I expose my skull. But I almost never do the things I want.

My only goal is to destroy myself and everything else.

And I spend at least five minutes out of every hour fantasizing about my bones breaking. (Usually my fingers).

I'm on the sun trying to extinguish it with my spit. I spit into the ocean and make it bigger.

My hands are numb after sleeping on them and I am pressing them into your head. It will be ok if my fingers break when I push them into your head because I won't feel it.

And the organs in my body would feel cheated if they knew the result of their work. This is an apology to my organs.

The sun is inside all the plants you eat and the animals that eat them and something will eat you and something will eat me. This is a promise.

Smell me. I am at least 1/3 dead.

Come to my room and get on your hands and knees and I will sleep on your back while you crawl around on the floor. We can take turns.

I am going to make a wig out of the dust that covers the floor. I will put the wig on my pillow and hug my pillow and be nice to my pillow.

My sink is full of dead flies and I don't empathize with anyone.

The price of every friendship is loss of time.

Having friends is narcissistic.

Climb onto your roof and yell at everyone that passes. You are safe on the roof.

I used a net to catch some bugs and I put the bugs into my

mouth and whispered them into your ear.

And you didn't hear what I said.

And you learned that wherever you take your stand, your back is turned on something else.

In the shower I cross my arms and let the water collect on the inside of my elbows and then the hairs on my arm sway in slow, underwater-motion and I imagine myself as a plankton with no hope or intention, navigating the hairs and hating the ground beneath me.

I am going to collect the eyes from all the dead animals and bugs I find and tape them to my eyes and kaleidoscope the world.

My spine is frozen spit and I dare you to break it in half.

Tonight I will know what I learned today and tomorrow I will forget it and learn it again.

SEVEN VERSIONS OF THE SAME VERSION

1.

I sat next to an old man on the bus yesterday. Our legs touched. We sat still for miles. A girl walked by us at a stop. The old man watched her pass then nudged me. He motioned for me to look too.

"Whew, huh?" he said. Then he turned and smiled at me.

I tried to think of something to say.

"Yeah I know," I said. "I'd definitely love to bite off one of her eyebrows and glue it to my upperlip. I've always wanted a pretty moustache. Or you know, just microwave a bowl of her blood—see what happens."

He readjusted himself in his seat and we sat staring forward for the remainder of the ride.

2.

The girl passed by and the old man elbowed me to look.

"Man, how bout it huh?" he said.

I smiled and nodded. Then I spoke loudly. "Yes, I agree with what I think you are suggesting. I would love to have sex with that girl. I don't know who she is but I think we can both agree that we should think about her body. I am aroused. How about you. Are you aroused, sir. Let's think about what we'd do. Let's think together. We can holds hands if you want, but that's up to you."

3.

The girl passes us and the old man puts his head in his hands. His head bounces in his lap with each subsequent turn and bump in the road.

4.

The girl passes us. As she passes, she temporarily blocks the window I've been watching, and the field outside it. I am angry that now I remember I am on a bus going somewhere and this somewhere will probably require something of me and I will either know or not know how to do that something and whoever is there, if even just me, will judge me capable or incapable. I'm now upset.

5.

The girl passes and leaves the bus and walks down the street and I never see her again. She will not think about me as she walks down the street into the millions of paths we will never choose in accord.

6.

I am almost asleep when the bus rounds a corner and sunlight comes through the window. The man next to me becomes rigid. He points to the cube-shaped piece of light on my shirt.

"Shit," he says loudly. "Oh shit. Get it off, quick." He leans back, pointing. The cube on my shirt grows. "Get it off—it's on you—get it off. Oh shit."

He crawls backwards to avoid the sunlight. I lose sight of him as the cube covers my face and I become too comfortable to stay awake.

"It's all over you—move," he yells. "Please."

His yells become more like pathetic whining and the whining sounds wet coming from the muscles in his throat.

The girl walking by is just one part of an endless number of things.

7.

I ignore the man and the girl. I feel a steady ringing begin in my ears. I am conscious of the ringing. It is all I can sense. It quiets my steps as I get off the bus. Somehow, I know it is my stop. I walk home. Somehow, I know all the steps. Someone is walking thirty feet or so behind me. I am afraid they are going to kill me. I am afraid but I shouldn't be, because no one would want to kill me. I repeat this to myself. "Don't be afraid. They're not going to kill you." I try to put the keys in my door quickly. The apartment is dark. I sit on my couch and worry about things that are not present. I let revolve in my head all the things I have to do, ultimately doing none of them until I begin to feel sleepy. I go to my room and lock the door. Halfway through the night, I wake up. I don't fall back asleep. Instead, I watch with eyes half-closed as the window in my room becomes lighter. It is almost time to get back on the bus.

CULTURE IS STUPID

I am watching you sleep and repeating the words, "You are my enemy" over and over until the steam collects on your face and your pores turn the steam into icicles of a whole new kind of sharpness.

Shake hands with your enemy to test their bones.

I am 24.

Living another 50 years seems impossible.

RESOLUTION

If I ever decide to shoot myself, I'll make sure to stuff my mouth with confetti, so it looks pretty for no one.

MY CAREER

I used to have an eight pack of crayons.
Then I bought a sixteen pack.
Then there were too many colors and I ran out of corresponding emotions.

Everybody likes me but that's because I'm a mirror lying face down in an empty field.

You know you're truly alone when you feel the need to tell someone about a nap you recently took.
You know there is nothing to say so let's take a nap.

And I am pissing on your grave.
I hope your mouth is open for this.

Today I will waste so much time the orbit of the earth will loosen, jettisoning our planet to freezing depths, far from the sun.
And I will not regret it.

I will claim you as my own, when everyone else disclaims you.
And I will not regret it.

And flies will eat your dead body.

My ideal date would involve painful silence.
My ideal date wouldn't involve me.

Nail me to your wall and I will make a sad face while I watch

you sleep.
I will give you a goodnight kiss but it will feel gross to you.
And I will not regret it.

Sometimes I wish I were a hair on your body because then I could be close to you but not have to say anything.
And sometimes I wish you were a hair on my body so I could cut you with a razor and not get in trouble.

All day I can only hear what sounds like a small annoyed kid playing a keyboard at a department store.

And if you find my skeleton in the forest, feel free to crack my ribcage in half and use the halves to rake up the dead leaves then burn them and smell the burn and say something you definitely don't mean.

I will pull patches of hair out of my head just like plants from dirt prepared by heavy rainfall.
And I'll call it maintenance because my field must remain undeveloped.
Because hair is bad ideas coming out of the skull.

There are too many emotions.
But I really only feel one, and it's, "I would kiss you goodnight except I'm allergic to assholes."

Outside of my head there is someone thinking, "Outside of my head there is someone thinking, 'Outside of my head there is someone thinking.'"

And your opinion never bruises me, it tickles.

All my fingers are criminals.
Only as beautiful as the worst thing I've done.

Personal eugenic scrutiny.
When the world holds its breath, I take mine.

I am the last breath of everyone you have loved.
I leave their body and blend with wind.
When I move, I flip over a leaf and an ant falls off the tip and slides down a wet blade of grass.

I set out little pieces of glass because I want the people who chase me to feel the trail beneath them.
I have no friends that have survived all circumstances.

I am good in bed (at sleeping).
Watch me sleep and see me wake up looking ungrateful.
I look at the ceiling and think, "There is no way to leave here."
And I am always right.

You are everything that you hide.
And I hug you to see behind you.
Or maybe to crush some vital organ.

This kind of scare is the worst.
This kind of scare involves us both forgetting everything.
This kind of scare makes us into confused people.
Both convinced we owe each other something.
But instead we become one aimless person.

And today, I have nothing to say and am proud of my decision not to try and come up with something.
I am waiting for whatever is mine.
It is better that way.
I have measured myself for the last few weeks and nothing has changed.
It is better that way.
I feel holy.

Somewhere in space is my first breath.

And you will become the people you hate.
You will remember them by becoming them.
Or no, you will become them by remembering them.
Their faces are little shields that prevent everyone else from becoming important to you.

WHAT I AM THINKING RIGHT NOW

I wonder if the man in front of me in line at the post office has any clue that I have been considering how many times I would have to stab the back of his skull with my pen, to break through and see his brain.

UNTITLED

I must be a piece of dust because I make your eyes water and you always try to get rid of me but I'm always coming back.

TOMORROW IS ON FIRE
AND I AM VERY YOUNG

Tomorrow is on fire and I am very young. Tomorrow I press your face into the ash of the old bridge. Tomorrow I push the ash of the old bridge into your eyes. Tomorrow I hate everyone I've ever heard of or known. Tomorrow is on fire and I am still very young. Tomorrow I will return and I am not a vindictive person, but I will point my finger in your face repeatedly, and my fingernail will make little moons on your face. The pressure will create little bruises around the moons, little clouds. Tomorrow is on fire and I am very young. You don't have to remember any of this, because I will keep saying it.

OUR MAIDEN NAME

First I produce a meaningful moment in your life then stop communicating with you so you feel hurt.

Then I do it as many times in a row as I can.

I can recite many things about myself that are true—like my address, name, and phone number.

Sometimes I recite these things to make sure I haven't become a completely different person.

But mostly I'm a cripple turning rusty padlocks.

Not one of them yet has opened to anything but another rusty padlock.

Here comes the creep of sun through my window again.

Which means I have to act like a human again.

Which means it's time to turn into a rusty padlock again.

There is no one to talk to and nothing to see.

Sleep tight.

ADVICE

A good thing to say after shaking someone's hand is: "Finally. I have always wanted to touch another human."

Another good thing to say is: "I will never be clean again" while looking idly at your hand.

GENITAL MUTILATION

In middle school, a kid in my class fastened a sharpened pencil to one of those rectangular pink erasers and set it on some other kid's seat. The other kid sat on the pencil and the pencil punctured his scrotum. He told us about it the next week when he came back to school. I didn't get a chance to ask him if one or both of his balls fell out (it was only later that I found out your balls are attached to something).

A PARTIAL LIST OF THINGS
I FEEL LIKE RIGHT NOW

A wrinkled hot dog spinning under a lightbulb in a gas station.

A pair of shoes stuck on an electrical wire.

The smell of a cough that an old man with lung cancer coughs into his hands.

Something important that was written on a chalkboard and then erased and you can still kind of see some of it.

A recently shit in diaper with a handful of sprinkles dropped on it.

Absolutely nothing.

SANDCASTLE

Me and you on a beach, the sand of which is my pulverized skeleton. I am making sandcastles with a shattered plastic bucket. I will enter your body and cough black ants with large abdomens into your bloodstream. You will cough the black ants out of your face and they will sink into the dust of my skeleton. The sand is my skeleton and your coughing turns up swirls. On your hands and knees, dead with my fluid, you will act as I made you.

I AM GOING TO JUMP-KICK YOUR FACE AND THEN KISS IT

I am going to jump-kick your face and then kiss it. I have been practicing my jump-kicks every day. I have been practicing my jump-kicks at least three or four times a day. That means I have performed more jump-kicks than the average human. That means when I jump-kick your face you will notice the power. That means when I jump-kick your face, it will mean more than if someone else did it. After I jump-kick your face I will kiss it. There will be many kisses—an amount that eventually becomes annoying and vaguely frightening. They will seem mad. And I won't even feel emotion while I'm kissing your face. It will just be something I am doing. I will kiss your face repeatedly. Mainly in the cheek area. But sometimes on the nose and sometimes on the forehead. And sometimes my mouth will be open. Sometimes my front teeth will touch your skin and it will be accidental. And I promise to open my eyes to assure you if that happens. When you feel teeth and then open your eyes, mine will already be open. But I will not stop kissing your face. The pleas to stop will not be obeyed. The next day you will wake up with your face against the pillow—your jump-kicked and violently-kissed face. It will hurt. You will touch it and feel how it hurts. I am practicing my jump-kicks—my kisses are already pretty good. You will get one of the former and many of the latter. You mean nothing and you are nobody. You are a crumb in my bellybutton. I am your universe.

I DON'T KNOW ANYTHING OR CARE ABOUT ANYTHING AND I SHOULD PROBABLY JUST SIT IN A FOLDING CHAIR AND DIE

Videotape your face and let it watch over you as you sleep.

Draw a picture of yourself and eat it.

Don't let culture lay a hand on you.

And don't own anything.

Don't envy anyone.

I put tape over your mouth and bang your head against the wall.

This is the perfect moment entering the perfect idea and vice versa.

Just let it pass.

UGANDAN HOOKER

My old roommate let one of his military buddies move in a while back. When the guy moved in, he spent three months on the living room couch staring at the tv. He ate chips and watched soap operas all day. I had a conversation with him one afternoon. He talked about Uganda where he was previously stationed. He said, "Yeah man, if a hooker gets pregnant there, they make her eat the baby right after it's born." I said, "I wish my mom was a Ugandan hooker."

DMV THING

At the DMV, while I waited for my new license to be printed, a lady walked in with a stroller. At the same time, I noticed a sign on the wall that read: No Eating or Drinking. I turned to the lady and motioned to her kid. "Excuse me ma'am, read the sign," I said. Then I realized she wasn't going to eat the kid, she was just watching it or whatever. But you never know.

HOLD HANDS WITH SOMEONE WHO HATES YOU

Praise is step one to death.

Don't look at me.

The next time you give birth to me I will curl up and strangle you before I am fully out.

And I encourage you to make my skull into your showerhead.

And I encourage you to enjoy the showerhead.

I'm looking for someone to spend time with.

But I can't afford too many hellos.

I WOULD FEEL BETTER ON EARTH WITHOUT YOU HERE

I should've worn underwear today. I should've called up a random number and asked them to come over today. I should've cut up the newspaper and made up new news today. I shouldn't even acknowledge that today is today. I should buy a model car set and assemble it and put it in my toilet and shit on it today. I should make up my own religion today. I should clean my boots. I should pry loose the slots of dirt from the treads and make a mannequin of myself. I should remember that I am going to die today. Not die today maybe, but remember it today. I should take a picture of myself to make sure I am real today. I should make sure.

I MAKE SHAPES

After I tear you in half I make shapes with your remains—distill salt from your body and use it to kill the plants growing on the better side of who you are—throw rocks at your statue—forget everything about you.

I have made marionettes out of my most painful anxieties and forced them into war and their blood has fed the earth's skin and grown the next war's field.

They'll come again as different shapes saying the same things. They'll come again and tear me in half.

I AM THE DICTATOR

Yesterday, we built a fort together out of a blanket and the couch and a few chairs.

The fort was flimsy but stayed up.

We brought a box of cereal underneath and laughed about how fun it was to be hidden.

We passed the cereal box back and forth and took turns eating it.

You told me a funny joke while I was eating and I purposely spit the cereal out on the floor of our fort.

The joke was: "I'm pregnant."

I swept the cereal back into order and put it back into the box.

The fort became really hot and sweat beaded around your mouth.

I put my fingers by your lips and did a little windshield washer motion.

I did it kind of hard.

Then there was quiet.

We did the wordsearch on the back of the cereal box and I found everything except for "cereal" "happy" and "hippo."

"Pillow fight," I said.

Then I hit you in the face with a pillow.

You laughed.

I said, "If the police come, don't tell them I hit you with a pillow. Tell them you fell, or I'll smash a hot lightbulb in your mouth."

You made a scared face.

"Just kidding," I said, and we laughed because for a second you thought I was actually going to burn your mouth.

I laughed loudly with my mouth wide so you could see my teeth.

Then we rolled around in the fort and laughed some more.

The fort kept coming undone and you kept fixing it.

You were good at fixing it.

We decided that freedom could be a dangerous thing in our fort utopia, so some form of political structure was needed.

I said plutocracy but you countered with dictatorship and I quickly said, "I call dictator."

You shrugged and allowed it because I was the dictator and if you fucked with me, that'd be it.

Our first task was to enact the systematic exclusion of all unwanted elements.

We created death camps.

One for everyone.

We killed everyone.

After the exterminations, you said you felt sleepy, and you lay down on the fort floor and fell asleep.

I put my hand on your stomach and it was warm.

I ate another handful of cereal and pulled out a bunch of plastic bags from my pocket.

I laid the bags out on the floor and straddled you.

I slid my forefinger and middle finger into your mouth along the crease of your tongue.

My fingers felt warm inside.

My stomach and groin tightened.

You continued to breathe and I put my mouth by yours and said, "I am the dictator."

Then I put my whole hand in your mouth and began pushing it down your throat.

Your throat was tight and smooth.

I got hard.

I kept my hand narrow.

The hairs on my hand and wrist slicked back and your throat bulged with my arm.

I pulled my hand back out with your heart in my hand.

I put it into a plastic bag.

I continued with the rest of your organs and your chest and abdomen sank in and grew wrinkled.

I did not find what I was looking for.

I sat back and touched each of the bags, wanting to see every little cell that beat life into you.

Wanting to take each organ to the sink in the bathroom and wipe all the blood off and trace the grooves with my fingers, pull back flaps and put my fingers in valves.

Smell them.

Know their shape and how they keep you alive to smile, or say something annoying.

Then I thought about filling up a leaf blower with nails and destroying each of the organs.

Would a leaf blower filled with nails do that, I thought. Would a leaf blower filled with nails kill organs.

I knew that inside your body there was something else.

I put my hands into the skin of your stomach like I was diving.

Then I pulled back two flaps and exposed your insides.

There was black water and leaves and twigs and little water-skipping bugs.

The black water drained and revealed a small body.

The arms were undeveloped, like featherless wings and the head resembled a bird-skull.

It was already dead when I scooped it out.

Sometimes you just have to relieve something of its surroundings for it to die.

I cradled the body and left the fort to the sound of your hollow breathing.

My shirt stuck to my belly with sweat.

I brought the body outside and set it in the alley, where the raccoons lived.

It was dark already.

I wiped my hands on my pants.

"I am the dictator," I said.

THE PRETTY MUCH DEAD LION

Today I walked to the library wearing shoes but no socks. By the time I got to the library, my heels and toes were bleeding. The library was closed. So I took my shoes off and sat on the steps for a while. Then I walked to the gas station across the street and bought some coffee and took a few napkins too. I sat on the curb outside and drank my coffee and wrapped pieces of the napkins around my bleeding toes. The wind blew against the blood-stained tissues and the tissues waved. They were my flags and I sat on the curb feeling like a very old lion with gray hairs on his face, not sure if he's even hungry enough to kill anything anymore.

PICNIC

In high school I was invited to a picnic at a forest preserve. Halfway there, I realized I had forgotten to purchase anything to bring to the picnic so I pulled over on the side of the road and grabbed a dead raccoon. I picked it up by the tail. All the hair stripped clean and it fell back to the ground. There were maggots crawling out of its ass. I left the raccoon where I found it and brought conversation and joviality to the picnic instead.

YESTERDAY

Yesterday I walked by a Chicago Police Department Training Headquarters. Three cops were walking down the sidewalk and one of them was gesturing to the others like he was cleaning the inside of a glass. I heard him say, "Yeah, the guy was like, 'What's that sound?' and then I was like, 'Relax, I'm putting your brain back in.'"

I SMASH MY SMILE AGAINST YOURS

And I fill my mouth with mud and put broken sticks in the mud and while you watch tv I bite you and bruise your arms and leave my name and address by the bruises so people know who gave them to you.

And I climb up trees and look out across fields and I feel fine eating candy by myself in a room and I have no ideas at all and I spit onto the sidewalk sometimes and watch ants eat it.

And I laugh at almost everything and your intestines are my umbilical cord and my umbilical cord is burnt shut and I am laughing right now and my laughing is my umbilical cord.

And I will hold your hand but I will have covered my palm in purple magic-marker so it makes it look like your hand is completely bruised.

And I smash my smile against yours and I'm not going to remember anything that happened today.

And I like to make out with the lines in your forehead when you frown at me.

And I want someone to think I am great for three seconds.

And I masturbate into the toilet and watch the clumps float like ghosts.

And I made my hand into a hospital and I made a replica of

your heart out of mud and now I am going to fix it.

And I feel embarrassed for long periods of time without knowing why and there are a lot of pubes around the rim of my toilet and I am starting to feel overrated as a human.

And I am a headless bird in the park on the cold, wet grass, and today the minutes pass me in slow, parade-float indifference.

And I only like things that have been beaten to death then resurrected.

And I put my head through the wall and fall asleep standing up.

And I want to break everything you own and then sit by the broken things and wait for you to return and when you do, I'll be like, "Yeah, I did all of this, how's it going."

And I hope you live for a hundred years so it takes you a hundred years to die.

And I never say hello to someone unless they already said hello to me and sometimes I act so nice to people it frightens them.

And I laugh so hard my face is ugly, but defined, like the stomach of an old woman who works out a lot.

And I don't have a face, my skull has acne.

And I put my head in a fish tank and let goldfish kiss my cheeks and swim between my eyelashes and I don't take myself seriously.

And I don't want to convince you of anything.

And I hope someone reads this and commits suicide.

And I put my hands behind my back and ask you to hit me and I say, "Please, please, please hit me."

And I lie down on your carpet so long that you think I will stay forever but I get up and I see the indentation in the carpet and I get jealous and say, "I am no longer needed here."

And I have been an embarrassment to everyone I've met and I will embarrass my enemies.

And I've lived in a lot of different places and I can't make friends because I can't form feelings.

And I am an idiot and the snow stuck in your hair smells like blood.

And when my nose itches, I scratch it on the sidewalk in front of your house and then when my nose is done being itchy I look at your house and feel shitty and alone.

And if you stay quiet I will lean over and put my mouth on your neck and say hopeless things that I really mean and I'm the one with the grenade heart.

And I like juiceboxes.

And I like picking apples out of trees and eating the apples while looking at the side of your breast coming out of a sweaty shirt.

And I pull grass out of the ground and throw it into the air.

And I am quiet while you're sleeping and I blow little breaths against your hair and think, "There is a storm, and I made it."

And it seems like every moment I'm alive I'm trying to recapture something good from a long time ago and I'm walking backwards to see if that good thing comes back and tries to jump on my back for me to carry it.

And I like to carry you on my back because your sweaty vagina feels good against me.

And I am the space between your knees when you clamp them together.

And I stare at myself while brushing my teeth and I laugh because I can reproduce.

And I put my finger in the barrel of your gun and the gun explodes and black dust covers your face and you've never looked better.

And I want to sled into a tree right now and forget everything about my life so far.

And I am the homeless man walking down the street and I am holding a pillowcase full of lightbulbs and no one talks to me.

And I rarely shower and I never use deodorant and: 'Knock knock.' 'Who's there.' 'Fuck you.'

And I was raised in a womb made of taffy.

And I shaved my pubes and braided them into a rope and hanged myself from my ceiling fan.

And I am a magician: I turned my apartment into a grave.

And I get so horny sometimes that I feel like acting nice to someone.

And I set your head down on the ground and jump on it with both feet.

And I measure your smile to see if I have improved.

And I have collected my bellybutton lint for a million years and I made you a very nice sweater and I sometimes just sit on my couch, naked, wearing tennis shoes and I have hair on my chest and face and head and armpits and feet and genitals.

And I am a clown who doesn't wear makeup.

And I am the reason I know white supremacy isn't true.

And I am on two broken legs walking up concrete stairs and above each one is another one and I keep thinking I am almost done.

And I always change things and then wish I'd left them alone.

And I sit in a room that has no history.

And when you die I will not cry about it or even celebrate it; I will watch it happen and look for something else to watch.

And half of the time I am in a conversation I feel like saying, "I have nothing to say" and the other half I nod politely.

And I'm willing to sit still and hear about everything you know and I want you to show me what one minus one equals.

And I hold what is mine in my arms like I will kill to protect it.

And I never liked you.

And the ceiling looks at us like prey and I fracture my skull against a light pole and I look up at the sky and say, "Please heal me."

And when I wake up tomorrow I will finish a thought that I began when I was three.

And I saw my reflection in a lake and I waited for it to freeze a little bit so I could break it with my boot.

And I have so many hugs for everybody it just makes me want to die and the hugs are crowded in my chest and they are beginning to hate each other.

And I stand with my face very close to yours and I stop breathing so your face will stay clean.

And I will survive anything.

And I am very sick.

And I sit in the sun long enough to burn my face and I peel the flakes off and place them on peoples' tongues like the eucharist.

And I put a condom over the Sears Tower.

And I break and burn bridges between two other people and I collect the ash and make concrete for new bridges.

And I have more fun with myself than anyone else.

And I like to lie because it is fun and also because confusing people is easy and everyone is so serious and I am a transvestite clown.

And I like your hips because I can sleep with my head on them.

And I jump up and down and hope my head will hit the ceiling of the sky.

And sometimes I say mean things to people, hoping their faces will break apart like an eggshell.

And I hate your heart because it spoils you.

And I put flower petals over my tongue and lick your neck and I sew my arms to a tree.

And I will build the ugliest things on earth using the earth to build them and I sit on my front lawn with a package of waffle cones and I scoop up dirt with the waffle cones and eat dirt out of them.

And I am either a newborn baby or a very old man and I am not upset when a car splashes me, because I'm on fire.

And I know different methods of self-destruction but none as intense as sitting still by myself.

And I hope we meet again so you can guess how old I am by the rings around my eyes and I hope we meet again so I can judge how much I've died according to your limp smile.

And I wish there was a god so I could send it a note that says, "Do you like me."

And I don't like being sad sometimes.

And I think my breath is fluorescent light and I feel the sun collect in my head and explode out into new stars that everyone hates and calls ugly.

And I know there is nothing to be upset about but it feels really good to be upset.

And I have no sympathy sometimes and I argue with myself all day and I'm a used condom stuck in someone's asshole.

And I lock myself in a room and do nothing.

And my blood is red chalk and I cough it out underneath the couch.

And I sleep on my couch and wake up with grooves in my face and I press my grooved face into the mud outside and create the map to a large city.

And I step on your face while you're sleeping and while you're awake I kiss your face and I am the most selfish person alive.

And I know tonight is part of the time I worry about but it is different because I use it to worry about what's coming and I know that what's coming is almost always disastrous and I say that the next day will be different but then end up doing nothing to effect that change.

And I want everyone to hate me because then I work best.

And I draw all the people I know on a chalkboard and sit by the chalkboard crossing them off one by one and I cover my hands with cellophane so nothing remembers me.

And I remember me better than anyone.

And I remember you how I need to and I am the old man sitting alone on a bench at the park looking at a newspaper but not really reading it.

And I trap bugs and then let them go.

And I say, "Peek-a-boo" and throw a knife at your house.

And I never say I'm sorry.

And I break my nose for something to do and I dig small holes and plant crayons and watch beams of color puncture the sky and I strangle you while you sleep.

And I threaten my neighbors with dirt smeared on my face and I bite off a fingernail and spit it into a spiderweb.

And, surprise, I like you way more than a friend.

And I rip out my tongue and put it in your belly and you starve to death.

And I am the best person ever and I hate everything I see.

And I dress up like a woman and jump from a tree and break my neck and lie there until the sun goes down and animals emerge and eat me.

And I cinch a belt around my head and crush my skull and use the pieces to pick my teeth.

And I talk until my mouth is dry and then I keep talking through the dry-choking.

And I buried an eyelash in drying concrete and I cut my finger on a book at the library and surprise now I'm immortal.

And I think about how tomorrow will be over soon enough and then I'll point at it and laugh at everything that happened.

PLEASE

Put your mouth around my ear so it sounds like I'm drowning in the ocean.

A VERY SHORT PLAY

A man and a woman are in bed in a room that is dark blue because the sun is setting. Water is hitting the window.

WOMAN: [looking out the window] Oh shit, it's raining again.

MAN: No.

WOMAN: [turns] What do you mean? I can see it.

MAN: Uh, I just set up the sprinkler while you were sleeping so the spray would hit the window. I didn't want you to leave.

I CLIPPED A RANDOM PICTURE FROM AN OBITUARY AND THEN ATE IT, HOPING I'D GIVE BIRTH TO THE REINCARNATED BODY OF THE PERSON IN THE PICTURE, BUT I DIDN'T, I JUST SHIT OUT THE PICTURE

I am going to clone myself then kill the clone and eat it.

I just reversed all your ceremonies—how do you feel.

I threw everything my throat had into the center of your mouth and turned your teeth into a broken and mud-splashed fence. You ate it like a greedy weakling. You make me hard.

In lieu of a condom I used a thoroughly chewed piece of raspberry gum when I fucked that dead moose over there (yes, that one over there, the one with the raspberry-smelling genitalia, no, over one, over one—yep, that one there.)

Goddamn, I have no feelings and the lines around my face already need to be cleaned again. I am a greedy weakling and I make myself hard.

I just reversed all your ceremonies again—that makes them the same as before.

I can trace my bloodline back to a stone at the bottom of the Atlantic Ocean and you know what, the best time to throw a lit match into someone's mouth is when they're laughing.

Light the wick that connects to the veins attached to your

heart. When you explode, the pieces of your body and your blood will line the wall. And I'll press my finger into the gore when it congeals so it will hold the impress of my fingerprint until the end of time when the lake in space eats the sun and everyone acts like there's a god, making sense of their real hero: themselves.

It's hard to determine if the emotion I'm feeling is mine or coming from somewhere.

For the past few hours I couldn't stop thinking about how it's impossible to sense my own weight so I thought about it and even tried lifting my arm and leg and other various parts but I was always right there.

The revenge of earth is reproduction.

It's killing me.

Actually no, my life never really got started.

I am going to board a freight train and it will take me somewhere that is not here. When it stops I will get off and look around and smile. It will be where I'm supposed to be.

ALZHEIMER'S DISEASE

When I get to hell I will save you a seat.

When you get to hell I will act like I don't know you.

SOMETHING I WORRY ABOUT

Walking home yesterday, I went between two streetlights. I watched the shadow in front of me and the one behind me move and align perfectly beneath. I worry that I am never going to learn anything or have anything important to say.

LET'S GO ON A DATE TOGETHER

Hello I am waiting in the parking garage for you and I have a bouquet of arm bones. Would you like to go on a date with me. You'll have to pay because I'm broke. Or we can go to my place instead. And I can comb your hair with the stem of a rose. And make faces behind your back. Turn you around and hug you. And slowly slip a knife through your back so it comes out the front and pierces me and we die connected.

I AM THE LAWNMOWER

Until I die, the world is the yard, composed of hands reaching up to shake mine.

And I am the lawnmower.

I LOVE YOU, YOU SHITHEAD

When I touch my face to yours, I think, "This is our first mistake."

I'M A NEGATIVE ASSHOLE AND THE EARTH IS A STUPID PLANET THAT SUPPORTS THE WEIGHT OF ITS OWN DESTRUCTION

Boo hoo. I am so sad.

I am in my room with the door locked, anticipating death.

There is no one in my room but me, and I am no one.

And I will welcome in whatever kills me.

The earth is stupid.

It is the only planet that supports the weight of its own destruction.

I am a negative asshole and the earth is stupid.

It supports me and I am ungrateful.

I will give the earth an unnecessary c-section and jump into the wound.

The earth will become sick with my body.

It will welcome in the thing that kills it.

Boo hoo. That makes me so sad.

I want to lie in the street and get run over repeatedly.

I want to put matches underneath my eyelids and blink tiny flames at someone.

I am a negative asshole.

And your crying is a song to me.

I will dismember everyone and sew millions of arms together to make a flag.

Then wave the flag over the sun and everything will change color.

Earth is stupid.

I will burn it down.

Then blacken my face with the ash.

Boo hoo. I am so sad.

And I think that anyone who likes me doesn't know everything they need to know.

Sit alone when you are happy. That way it won't spread.

Cry into a bottle and put a rag in the bottle and light the rag on fire then throw it at the sky. The sky will melt and drown us.

This is the captain.

I have made a home on a stupid planet.

Whoever runs my brain is doing a shitty job.

And I support the weight of my own destruction.

The way home is beneath your feet.

The way home is to drop dead.

And be done.

I don't have any feelings and your crying is a song to me.

I want to sit and watch you cry.

I'm like reverse-god.

And I'll give you an unnecessary c-section.

And my hands won't hate their work.

Like reverse-god.

And I'm in my room, slowly becoming garbage.

My cum smells like flower compost.

And it is in you.

And you are a skeleton.

And my cum makes holes in your skeleton.

And you support the weight of your own destruction.

You slowly die.

And my hands don't hate their work.

Welcome in whatever kills you.

Sit alone in your room with your door locked.

Anticipating death.

Sit alone. And welcome in whatever kills you.

The way home is to drop dead.

And be done.

Boo hoo. That makes me sad.

THE WORST PART ABOUT ANYTHING
IS THAT IT WILL BE OVER

I am going to cook my hand over the burner on the stove and eat all the meat off, leaving only the bone. Then I am going to pin my skeleton hand against the ground with my knee and break it off at the forearm. I am going to take the skeleton hand outside and stick it into the ground, planting a different kind of flower. Still waving, still eating sun. This is saying goodbye. I am going.

DEAD HORSE

If I ever find a dead horse, I am going to beat the fucking shit out of it. I will beat the shit out of the dead horse until all the bones in my fingers, hands, wrists and arms are broken. Then I will beat the dead horse with my feet and let my broken arms flail uncontrollably like a violent sprinkler. If I ever find a dead horse, I am going to beat the fucking shit out of it.

FROWNS NEED FRIENDS TOO

I HEART UNENDING PARANOIA

One day I want to wake up to someone telling me s/he hates me. I want that person to follow me around all day, telling me how much s/he hates me. That person can tell me as many times as seems necessary and in any way s/he wants. At night I will cook that person dinner so s/he doesn't get too weak to keep telling me about hating me. And I will try to make sure that person gets enough blankets when we're going to sleep, so s/he doesn't get too cold to tell me how much I am hated. And I will try not to pull the blankets off in the night (even if it's totally accidental (and if I accidentally do pull off the blankets, I hope that person is not an asshole about it (or at least I hope that person is not too upset to continue telling me how much I am hated))). I need to hear it for at least a week straight to return to normal.

PUBERTY

I believe you can destroy a city with a somersault, provided the city is small enough and provided you don't have a bad back.

I believe you can trample your friends if you don't like them and I believe you can trample them or anything else in a way that makes it seem like that's not what you're doing.

I believe that no one is guilty of anything.

I believe all material objects are made of small green circles that resemble blood cells and I believe that those small green circles all look the same. And I believe you are one of the small green circles.

I wouldn't argue with someone who said I was smaller than outerspace, no.

Because I'm destined to never talk to a certain amount of the population.

That is true about you.

That is true about the rest of the population.

You can cut out a small cube of air and use it as a pillow and you can see things while you are sleeping that will make you lots of scared.

But who doesn't like a dumb scared motherfucker.

DURING SEXUAL INTERCOURSE I ENVISION MY OWN BRUTAL DEATH

The other day I went for a walk and while I was at an intersection I saw a man wearing colorful shorts.

I said, "I like your shorts."

He looked down and then back at me and paused.

He said, "Yeah, these are like, my favorite shorts. That's why I wear them so much."

I said, "Yeah, I can see why. If those were my shorts I would wear them a lot too."

He nodded and then turned and looked at the stoplight.

It was the most successful conversation I have ever had.

I thought, "Just quit now."

CONSTANT STARING

Sometimes I can't sleep because I'm thinking about all the people I have disappointed.

Sometimes I can't remember who those people are but I'm sure they are there.

Sometimes I can't sleep because I'm thinking about new and better ways to disappoint people.

Sometimes I worry there is no one left to disappoint.

I CAN IMITATE A FLOOR

When I get what I want, no one else will.

And wherever I stand, the world gets my weight.

I am meditating on the idea of my own throat cut down to the spine.

Today I walked by an old lady on the street and she said, "Kill yourself."

Shhh, no one is breathing anymore, no one is awake.

When others get what they want, what you want is changed.

I WOULD DRINK A MOUTHFUL OF WATER THAT IS A MOUTHFUL OF WATER A THOUSAND OTHER PEOPLE HAVE PASSED FROM MOUTH TO MOUTH

There is an I.V. of the times I have thought, "I don't know what I'm talking about" and it is swelling my veins.

I want to fall in front of you and make you laugh.

Everything is exactly the same.

Everyone is describing the same thing.

The only difference is what scrapes what.

A big rock becomes a small rock becomes a big rock becomes something you throw into the air becomes something you hope lands on you and kills you.

When I say mean things I am apologizing quietly in my head. And isn't it great how quiet some things are.

I like to be constantly half-damaged. I like to scrape myself and then apologize.

I am sorry I have made more people than have made me cry.

No, I'm not sorry.

How many times have you held the answer in and felt like a

shitty little petty motherfucker champion.

A picture of the back of my head proves that other places exist and that I can be wrong.

And I am teenaged every few minutes.

The only son of a puddle's crater.

Look how huge I am.

Arms strong from waving goodbye to assholes.

NO-JOY HEADLESS ADOLESCENT

It is impossible to dislike someone you see sleeping.

MY ROOM IS NOT AN EYELESS SHAPE THAT IS TRYING TO EAT ME

My room is not an eyeless shape that is trying to eat me.
My room is not an eyeless shape that is trying to eat me.

I WASTE TIME BY THINKING ABOUT THE FUTURE IN DETAIL

The next time I put my weight on you will be the next time I scratch my facial hair into your neck and chest will be the next time red lines form from the scratching—composing a pretty picture—will be the next time I remember that I am going to be alive for a long long time will be the next time I remember that the meantime is meant for changing everything into something that retains the marks of my intervention will be the next time I put my weight on you.

BE LAUGHY

The underwear I want is the kind made from barely-slept eyelids.

The kindness I have is the kind pulled from deep inside the couch, where you reach and sometimes your hand gets poked.

The new facial features I made are the kind fashioned from muscles unwrapped from a sleeping ribcage.

The hand I want is the one I have and the things that go inside are what's missing.

The thing I want is what misses me.

One of us is an earthworm in a chewed-on papercup full of sand.

And the other is the person watching.

ABUSIVE ROMANCE-PARTNER

There is no night and day there are only small naps.

There is no way to understand anything there are only nods

There is no holding hands there is only making sure the other doesn't run.

There is no idea there is only saying something one of us already said but forgot about.

There are no naps there are only blinks.

There are no blinks there are only small rips in sight.

There is no fun there is only me not saying anything.

There is no floor there is only feeling like you can't go more below.

There is no washer and dryer in my apartment building and that sucks fucking balls.

There are no fingers there are only smaller pieces of your arm.

There are no arms there is only your body trying to expand without your permission.

There are no endings there is only not wanting to continue.

CHICAGO ASSHOLE ALL-STAR

Is good feeling to just stare back at someone who has failed to make you laugh. Is good feeling.

Is ridiculous that I have to wear clothes everywhere.
Is ridiculous.

I have been alive for thousands of days.

Right now I am sweaty and I feel like I have given up.

And the only way to sleep is to not be anything else.

More of my time is spent thinking about how I could die at any moment rather than setting goals and achieving those goals.

And my goal is to be found in someone's pool.

Being dead will be the easiest thing I do.

I am not accomplishing anything—my feet are shovels and all my sperm are tailless.

Is good feeling.

THE NAP

At the grocery store today I saw a very huge woman on a motorized vehicle.

There were kids running circles around her.

When I got outside with my groceries there was snow falling and I knew the snow was disappearing when it hit the ground.

I also knew that I was at the part of the nap where I realize the nap is long. Very long.

I was at the part of the nap where I realize the nap is long and that it will end itself without my permission.

UNDYING ACCIDENT-BIRTH PULLED FROM BETWEEN BROKEN LEGS

My fingernails would make great shingles for a very small person's house.

And my chest hair would make great carpeting.

My teeth could make shovels to overturn small pieces of earth and I hope a tree grows over my grave and the roots strangle my skeleton.

I have a videotape of my conception—it is proof no god exists.

Just kidding.

I am a human with its eyes closed. And I regret everything I do.

My face is proof.

Gross.

So gross.

PERSON IN A WHEELCHAIR ON A TRAMPOLINE

I don't care if it takes me the rest of my life I am going to spit on my feet until I float away from the planet into space where there's no one to talk to and nothing to do.

You can be a miniature god if you shoot my boiling head and kill it.

Shoot my boiling head—I feel too stupid to move.

My plaque deposits become horns when I shove them deep into my forehead. Still look the same.

And I can kill anything that is smaller than my mouth or hands.

And I can become small enough to represent myself as a secret.

Yuh huh.

Everyone is describing the same thing.

SOME PEOPLE HAVE PERSONALITIES THAT ARE COMB-OVERS

1. While I was waiting for the bus I put my hand into my pocket to get some change but my fingers went through a hole in my pocket and I accidentally touched my own leg. It felt horrible. I hope that never happens again.

2. While I was waiting for the bus I put my hand into my pocket to get some change but my fingers went through a hole in my pocket and I touched air. My leg was gone. I looked at my hand. My hand was gone. My legs and feet were gone. I was a rock. Some wind blew me into the street and I made the street heavier and I forgot about the bus.

3. While I was waiting for the bus I put my hand into my pocket to get some change. I took my hand out and it was filled with ants. "That's where I put those," I said. The bus pulled up and I stared at it, ants falling out of my hand.

4. While I was waiting for the bus I put my hand into my pocket to get some change. A person walked up to the bus stop and said, "There will be room on the bus for us both because we are nothing." I nodded.

5. While I was waiting for the bus I put my hand into my pocket to get some change and I forgot where I was and what I was doing and I looked at a cloud for help but it said nothing.

PISS-BUSH

I can make a gift for you that is a snowball in a brown paperbag and I can make a gift for you that is confetti cut from lamplight and I make gifts like that, that's all I do.

I woke up facedown in my pillow and I thought the world was gone and I became a millionaire but I was wrong and now I regret throwing out all of my underwear and socks.

Being alive for a whole year seems like it deserves a commemorative plaque I think.

Sometimes if I think about breathing it becomes hard to breathe and I almost pass out.

Definitely best not to think about anything.

Definitely good to watch someone cry.

If I knew what I was doing I would stop doing it.

After I figure out how to eliminate people, I figure out how to miss them.

And a small town can become a big field if you destroy it thoroughly.

And my face hurts from frowning.

I apologize.

People act according to how many people they want to visit their grave or just think about visiting their grave.

A car crash breaks your arm but sitting still breaks your spine and some things explode without moving.

Underneath each of my fingernails are friends—on their backs with their arms and legs pointing upward—waiting to be turned over to crawl off.

Win friendships with a bad mind. Do that.

I guide a river into your sleeping ear and it comes out the other end a different color.

You get one long chance to be a failure and the fewer times you fail the bigger that chance gets.

Have a nice night and be pleased by rupturing your own blood cells.

I can't believe I am this close to the ground.

I CAN'T THINK OF A TITLE FOR THIS BECAUSE MY ATTENTION SPAN IS DISAPPEARING (NOT JOKING, I'M CONCERNED)

I have sex dreams where I hold someone and I don't have sex with them.

I have a feeling that other people are ruining my mind.

And when I visit someone it's fun to just leave when that person goes to the bathroom or goes to get something.

We're lucky no one can stand themselves individually otherwise we wouldn't be needed.

I got up a second ago and accidentally hit my finger on the doorframe and now my finger feels broken.

There is no way to be comfortable anymore.

No more fun from now on.

BE JEALOUS

I promise I will be more professional with hurting your feelings horribly and I promise when I point my finger it will have my whole boneframe behind it. I promise I am going to keep you, and give you enough water and food and care. I don't know what I am doing. But I promise I will make my head professional. I promise to be mean. There are endless ways to ruin a house but making it feel bad about itself is the quickest and most professional. Everything I think or have thought is true. Weak things collapse. Tell your friends how much you dislike them. I promise I don't know what I'm doing but I'm a professional. I promise there are more examples of how to mistreat people than anything else. I promise to professionally make you an example.

HEIL ME!

Sorry I clipped your fingernails too short but it's hard to do with scissors—please don't be mean.

You can put your fingers in my mouth I have a feeling that will make them better.

When I lick the pulp beneath your nails you will feel better and maybe I will too.

And maybe your pulp will teach my tongue new things about being soft.

Sorry about cutting your fingernails too short but I still like you a whole lot.

Sorry, but some hugs are terrible. They leave me feeling like I got soaked on my way somewhere and I like, only halfway dried off before the day was over.

What I'm trying to say is, I need to build a real forcefield around me to replace the fake one.

FRUIT SNACKS

Don't touch me—my skin is boiled by heartbroke-flies dropping tears.

I will never see all myself at once.

I will never see most of my organs.

I will never surgically remove anyone's cancer.

I will never be a greatgrandmother.

I will never teach anyone how to do complex math.

I will never give birth.

I will never jumprope off a mountain.

I will never perform a magic trick that makes someone admire me.

I try to make people laugh so for a period of a few seconds I have done nothing wrong and I owe nothing.

And the blackest color is behind your eyes.

I will never make a map of anything.

I will never stop making lifesize maps of the holding cell you make for me in your bad hopes.

I was eating some cereal and one of the marshmallows stuck to my lip and then it fell off and went beneath the couch and I am not going to look for it I think I am going to leave it there alongside the muscles I use to hold up my eyelids yeah man.

Fail in public like a petty motherfucker champion.

Fail and let it make you hard.

Yes I get hard when I put my hand on your knee.

Yes you get mad when I put my hand on your knee.

Yes I get hard when you are mad.

Yes nothing gets me hard anymore.

MY LITTER-SKULL

If you don't kill your bad thoughts, your bad thoughts will kill you.

It's the same with your pets and the same with all your relatives I guess.

SOMETHING TELLS ME I'M GOING TO DIE IN AN ALLEY

When your hand is a field it will make many things.

When your hand is a field it will be covered in dirt.

When you stand face to face with the things you've made but do not like, it will define you in some way.

And when your hand is a field your tongue is a cloud.

When there's nothing left to say I will go to sleep and you will never hear from me again.

The moment I have gained some importance in your life I will be gone—that's natural.

Yesterday I saw a squirrel run out into the street and a car ran it over.

The squirrel kind of tried to run away but just fell down.

Then the squirrel twitched once, like it was doing a sit-up.

Then it was still.

I'm glad I saw that because otherwise I would've had nothing to think about while I was sitting on the train this morning, waiting to twitch once, then be still.

CHESTHAIR TOUPEE

When someone says something to me and I'm not listening and it looks like they want a response, I act startled and point behind them and say, "Oh shit—get down."

Then I run away.

THE EARTH SNIFFED PAINT WHILE IT WAS PREGNANT WITH ME

I have to find a bed where no one will find me.

No one can know where my real bed is.

I saw a pile of leaves today and thought, "No one will find me here. Here is good for a bed."

I thought the same thing about this girl's hood while I was in line at a store but then I remembered she would probably fall over if I slept in her hood and I said, "Oh yeah" out loud and she turned and looked at me.

Everything you care about is easily lost or has to die off and you won't know how it happens until it happens.

You don't have to forget everyone you meet but you can if you want .

If you want, no one can find you.

NOT WEARING UNDERWEAR MAKES ME HORNY

The main difference between me and a caterpillar is that I will remain a disgusting bug.

The main difference between me and a pedophile is that I don't have a moustache.

Last night I sat on the curb out front of my apartment and I looked back at my apartment and realized it wasn't my home and I looked at the moon and pointed at it, making a gun motion with my finger and thumb and I smiled with one eye closed, repeating the words, "Hello, I am a bad enemy to have and an even worse friend."

My back hurts today. Put an ice cube in your mouth for a little bit then lick my back.

I cover myself in mirrors and I make no friends.

When I make friends I cover them in mirrors.

Every time I open my mouth I melt the things in front of me and every time I draw x's over my eyes I fool other people into not introducing themselves.

When you hear yourself saying something, make sure you hear yourself as a complete enemy.

When you wake up today, treat the first thing you see like a complete enemy.

Nothing can absolve the day.

When you touch the ceiling of your scared life look at your fingers and remember the color.

Absolve the day and feel huge.

I SAW A DEAD BODY ON THE CORNER OF ASHLAND AND ROOSEVELT AND I WALKED BY IT AND THERE ARE SIXTEEN VERSIONS OF WHAT HAPPENED

1. I was walking on the sidewalk and saw a body lying in the street with a blanket over it. There were police everywhere. I think maybe the police could've situated a bunch of tissues or pillows underneath the blanket just to fool me but I don't think they would do that.

2. I walked down the street and saw a dead body lying in the street with a blanket over it. I thought about getting underneath the blanket too but I knew I wouldn't be able to stop laughing when the police loaded me into the ambulance.

3. I saw the dead body. There were a lot of people but no one was talking to each other. I crossed the street and there was a man at the other side. I looked at him and said, "It's really cold out." He said, "Yeah." And I walked past him.

4. I walked past the dead body and after I was out of sight the dead body disintegrated and floated upward in small screams that no one could hear.

5. I walked up to the dead body and the police. I looked at one of the policemen and said, "If you want, I can lift it up and put it way high up in a tree so it's out of everybody's way." The policeman said, "For some reason the first thing I thought after you just talked to me was, 'Fuck you.'" I thanked him and told him to come get me if he needed someone to throw the dead

body way up high in a tree.

6. The dead body wasn't really there I just mistook a really big puddle for a dead body.

7. I walked up to the dead body and tried to tickle its feet. It didn't move when I tickled its feet. A cop said, "I tried too—nothing."

8. I folded the dead body up when no one was looking. I put the folded dead body in my pocket. I walked away. I was so excited to see it I left it in my pocket and touched it once in a while to make sure it was still there. It was always still there. Now I don't even check.

9. I saw the dead body and walked across the street. I passed a girl on a cellphone. I think she was trying not to make eye contact with me. I understood that and appreciated that. I looked at my feet and forgot what I was supposed to be doing for the next couple of decades.

10. I walked up to the dead body and I said, "Hello, how are you." The dead body said nothing and we became best friends.

11. When I saw the dead body I turned to the policeman and said, "What do you call this again." The policeman said, "That is called a human." I said, "Oh yeah, thanks." And I walked away and I knew what a human looked like. I saw them everywhere.

12. I walked up to the dead body and the policeman and I played a few games of tic-tac-toe on the dead body and the policeman kept winning because he kept taking the middle spot like a cheating motherfucker.

13. I walked up to the dead body and lay down next to it and I put my arm around it and said, "What time do you have work tomorrow, honey."

14. I stopped next to the dead body. A policeman looked at me. I smiled and said, "You will do just as good a job as this person is doing, don't worry." The policeman said, "I am the same thing standing up."

15. I walked up to the body. I looked at it. I bent down and scooped some water from a puddle. I put the water up to the dead body's mouth. Nothing happened. I thought, "I am going to go watch tv," and then I walked away and my hand was cold and wet.

16. I came up to the dead body and I looked at it. I could tell where the nose was under the blanket and where the mouth was too. When I tried to imagine more, it became impossible. I wanted to lift the blanket but I knew how cold the body would be without the blanket. I didn't feel anything else. I didn't care. I still don't care. Everyone is fine where they're at.

A CAREER OF LOOKING TIRED

When I wake up, I stay completely still and say, "Yayyyy" for as long as I can with one breath.

Yesterday I acted like the lightbulb in my room was the sun and outside my door there were too many evil people waiting for me, so I didn't leave.

I did good acting.

I did good acting for as long as I could with one breath.

WAITING FOR SOMEONE TO LOOK AT ME AND SAY, "WHAT'S WRONG" (THEN I BLACK OUT, REMEMBERING NOTHING)

The people who hate you are strong when you misstep.

I can stand completely still.

I can never move again.

I will become the last warm blood cell in the not-breathing and useless you.

Teach me to trace the shape of the last warm blood cell in the not-breathing and useless you.

Teach me to stretch the last warm blood cell over my head and sleep on the ozone layer using my hands as pillows.

Am a good boy.

Am sitting in an alley behind a grocery store eating an apple and I don't believe anything.

If you touch my face you will know exactly what I look like.

Am your hero.

I like pineapple juice and I also like snowflakes.

No one is my hero.

A broken pencil in a two-inch puddle is my hero.

The broken pencil in the two-inch puddle stands completely still.

Am the broken pencil.

"SUCKS ASS" WOULD BE A FUNNY WAY TO DESCRIBE SOMEONE'S HAIRCUT IF ASKED FOR AN OPINION

I should wear a nametag everywhere I go—it would remove one more thing I have to say.

I don't laugh at anything anymore.

Someone stole my carbon copy and is making it do dumb shit.

And I'm just watching, laughing.

I LIKE WHEN SOMEONE ELSE SCRATCHES MY CHEST

I have copies of your dental record and I cover my window with them so your teeth and their roots are the first thing to touch my face when I wake up.

My face hurts from frowning.

And my hands are swollen from getting mad then doing nothing but sitting on them.

I am walking around and pushing the buildings of Chicago into Lake Michigan.

Would you be sad to see the building you're in become a boat. No you wouldn't.

I spend too much time worrying.

But I feel close to accomplishing the greatest feat of human quietness. I'm so close.

There is so much time I think I will prove it by doing nothing today.

Honestly, I am worried about falling in the shower.

Honestly, worried can be a nice feeling.

Honestly, somewhere in a cave there is a drop falling off a

stalactite and it is looking around to see if anyone saw what it just did.

I am always trying to prove that I'm not a waste of time.

And if you smile, I win.

There is nothing that will still hurt my feelings. Nope.

My eyes float up and split in half along the sockets and I sit eyeless, seeing things I can't touch.

Best friends are flimsy.

I am not interested in being a good-looking human anymore.

If you smile I'm a good-looking human.

I win.

SCREAMING FACE

I saw a man fall while he was trying to get into his friend's car. He lifted his arm up and it was broken. It looked like he was screaming but for some reason I couldn't hear any screaming. He made a screaming face and his friend helped him up. The friend kept trying to put his coat over the man with the broken arm. It seemed like the friend was trying to make the man with the broken arm disappear into the coat. I would like to be able to make people disappear into my coat, but I wouldn't know where to start. True. It's like I'm always making a screaming face.

SOME SHIT ABOUT WHAT I'D DO WITH TIME TRAVEL

I'd go to the date of my death and take of picture of my face right before I died and then frame it and go back to the present and stare at the picture.

I'd go to my grave in the future and just sit there until I died, to confuse people.

And right now I am sitting and looking at the wall, drinking a glass of water and staring, and I don't ever think I am better than anyone else.

Not ever.

DON'T CONFUSE THE MARCH OF THE THING YOU HATE FOR HOW IT BLINKS ITS EYES AT YOU

When I grow up I want to be a fireman. When I grow up I want to be my own family. When I grow up I want to die. When I grow up I want to be left alone. When I grow up I want to be asleep on the floor of an empty apartment. When I grow up I want to have accomplished my present goal of distancing myself from everyone I know. When I grow up there will be no one who remembers anything about me. When I grow up I will barely remember anything about me and I will remember lying in bed guessing when the next lightning bolt will light up my room and show me I cared about this at one point but could never care again. Maybe that. When I grow up I want to be a middle aged man who people pity when they see him walking around, looking tired and ugly and never nice enough to want to get to know. Maybe that.

UNTITLED

The engraving on a nickel or dime or any coin should be someone sleeping on a couch with his/her winter jacket over him/her like a blanket, trying to avoid what comes through the blinds.

BECAUSE YOU KNOW YOU'RE AVOIDING GOING SOMEWHERE BUT YOU DON'T EVEN KNOW WHERE YET

Every person is an only child.

Practice how to discontinue your siblings.

I avoid entering my apartment if I know someone else is looking because I'm paranoid about people knowing where to find me.

But seriously, how are you today.

I got ok force and I use it on myself.

It takes a long time to patiently drop water onto a napkin one drop at a time so all the drops touch sides but it's worth it to create that kind of togetherness. It's worth it.

Right now you are looking at something that at some point I looked at and we are not going to die at the same time probably but the space in between deaths will be small compared to all known time and the idea of time in general.

The downside of smiling is smelling your own body cavity— the infected tissue inside on vacation that gives you a few decades of movement.

And if I reacted to other people the same way I react to myself I wouldn't have any friends.

I don't have any friends now but it's for different reasons I think.

In the morning when I'm hard, I don't think about anything while I wait to get soft.

I wait to get soft.

THE QUICK VERSION OF HOW TO BE SUCCESSFUL

Find a small place no one else can find.

THE INTRUDERS ARE REAL AND THEY ARE GOING TO KILL ME IF I STOP PROTECTING MYSELF

I sleep with my sheet wrapped all the way over my head except for my mouth because I am convinced the intruders will kill me if I see them.

I get sweaty when I am sleeping but being sweaty is better than getting killed by the intruders.

I sleep so they can't kill me.

But I won't yell if they do.

I don't know what I am doing but lately I have noticed that I don't listen to the first couple of words people say to me and then I have to like, catch up so I can understand them and reply.

Inside a big lake is a smaller lake.

Insider me is a bigger me.

Inside me is a much much smaller me that acts like it's huge.

And when your body shakes and the air in front of you says nothing and there is no one to confirm that you still make a difference, you will reach into your chest and the dust and crumbs will greet you.

LOVE STORY

I went to the gas station tonight to buy a drink. I had to wait behind a girl filling up her cup at the fountain. She sipped some of the drink and put a lid on it. I said, "If you were my girl, I'd buy you the 36oz. size fountain drink. You could have it all. You could have the biggest fountain drink in the world. We could die in it." She sipped her 22oz. sized drink and looked at me and said nothing. Then she walked away and I wondered what went wrong because I knew I pronounced everything right. It is hard to pronounce things right.

DEATH

I want to say, "Them's fighting word" to someone after they ask me what time it is.

My whole life is that feeling you get when you are at someone's house and you have nothing left to say—you have only been repeating things that already happened.

I keep a chart of the times I have accomplished complete silence.

When I walk down the detergent aisle at the store I can't breathe and I get drastic, looking around for help.

I will not make you feel ugly I will show you how fun it is to be a human. And how to not-want to be anything anymore.

Good.

IN THE LAST TWO YEARS I HAVE TALKED TO ANIMALS OR MYSELF MORE THAN I HAVE TALKED TO OTHER HUMANS

There is enough blood in my body to flood a dollhouse or at least fill up an average sized sock.

Tie your hands to your feet and lick your own genitals.

You can reward yourself.

We are going to be friends or enemies—I don't have neutral engagements.

To begin, melt your relatives and nationality.

Melt your fucking nationality.

I would like it if someone put me in a cardboard box and then taped the cardboard box up tight and lit the box on fire, kicking the box repeatedly.

Make me a dot-to-dot of your sudden dislike of my voice.

And make sure you do as little to help out other people as you can.

Make up a name for yourself.

And make up everything you ever tell anyone.

Your sweaty armpits are my pillows.

I scratch my face in your sharp, three day un-shaven armpits and feel drug-empty.

My sperm have misshapen heads.

And I don't contribute anything. True.

Being worthless is hard work, but you love everything about me.

Puzzles are shitty because you only end up putting together a picture that's already completed on the front of the box.

When I'm spending time with other people, I can only think about the moment when I'll get up to leave and how it will be signaled.

And yes, being asleep is fine, but it always ends.

And yes, sleep is fine but I'll stick with staying inside and looking out the backdoor or looking out the peephole at the hallways, wondering where all the people are going and why they aren't asking me to come with.

WHAT IT IS, MOTHERFUCKERS

The earth goes bald of all humans.
And it is impossible not to become a tradition.

I HAVE A PROBLEM WITH RANDOM LAUGHING

The weapon in your hand is more important than your hand or your heart or your head.

I want you to make me so upset I pass out. Then take turns.

I am aiming at the weapon in your hand, not your hand or your head or your heart.

Hold me and I will aim at myself. And then take turns.

We make a great team because you need someone to not-look at and I like to feel needed.

My spine is strong from holding up a huge hologram of pure shit.

YOUR EMBRYO

Break your embryo open and drink from it.

I pushed your face into the fabric of the couch and said, "I love you."

You looked one-day dead.

You smelled newborn.

We blended our cells together then ended.

I forcefed you smegma with my fingernail and we sat naked on the tile floor—carefully avoiding every emotion.

We became normal again.

I told you I was afraid to sleep because my dreams reproduced real life.

And I knew you weren't listening, so I said:

Everyone hates you and it is perpetual day.

Everyone hates you. It is perpetual day.

Everyone hates you.

Everyone hates you during perpetual day.

It is perpetual day and everyone hates you.

It is perpetual day and everyone hates you today.

Don't be afraid of sleep. Carefully avoid every emotion.

It is today and everyone hates you.

It is today and everyone hates you today.

It is perpetual day.

Break your embryo open and drink what is inside.

You will never recover from how you treat yourself.

And personality is something that is gone when you start talking.

My body leaves its outline on the ground forever.

Carefully avoid every emotion. Everyone hates you.

BIPOLAR IDIOT

And you will define yourself by hating your surroundings and hoping it's mutual so you don't look petty.

Standing directly in front of someone is a way to become the surroundings.

I pray you embarrass your enemies.

The less you say the more cleanly you die off this earth.

You become surroundings.

DICKHOLE

Being dead is the new alive.

I pulled my arm off and sharpened the bone and cut the earth in half and slept between the halves.

And volcanoes will return my blood.

And all earth is the hardened form of the dead-me.

And all earth controls the still-alive.

Sometimes when people talk to me, I feel like I just hit the garage door button and I need to run quickly to get out.

When you're sleeping, I put my fingers on your face and smear it around like a finger-painting.

But I make sure I put it back together the right way before you wake up.

My fun lasts forever.

An entire bottle of perfume washes my face.

Natural causes, they will not kill me.

My fun lasts forever in weakening approximations behind old cells.

If you tell me you love me, I will keep saying, "What?" and acting like I genuinely didn't hear you until you hate me.

And that will be fast.

Burn your photo albums. They don't know you.

Today I am broken in half, staring up at the sky that raised me and it is bruised and split, spilling into my mouth, which I try to keep closed.

I want to cut your belly open and dip my feet in, like someone relaxing at the pool, on vacation.

But who knows.

Who knows how I will vacate.

Being alive on earth makes me feel like a spoiled kid at a sleepover at someone else's house.

WANTING OTHER PEOPLE TO THINK LIKE YOU IS DUMB

Two people were murdered outside my apartment last night. I think I would like the job of taking names off mailboxes. Or throwing the ashes of cremated strangers into the air. I think I would like the job of not remembering anything. Or trying to help other people forget things. I be tired as a motherfucker, that is true.

I'M NOT GOING TO CHANGE
MY CLOTHES TODAY

I'm not going to change my clothes today.

I'm not going to be upset about eating by myself—I'm going to anticipate it positively.

I'm not going to change my clothes today.

I'm going anywhere today except for the bathroom and maybe even then I will stay there.

I'm not going to be surprised by anything.

I'm not big enough to control myself at all times—I'm small enough to hate every time I forget.

I'm not going to share anything.

I'm not going to fill up a brown paperbag with water because I know that won't work.

I'm not going to fill up a brown paperbag with water because there has to be a better way to build a friend.

I'm not going to change my clothes today.

I'm not going to allow myself the same kindness I allow others.

I'm not going to turn the lights on in my apartment from now on because I don't want to accidentally highlight my grave.

I'm not breathing I'm trying to inside-out myself.

I'm not going to change my clothes ever.

I'm not going to ask anyone how they're feeling.

I'm not going to change my clothes today.

I'm not going to lie, I feel like I need to become inside-out and touch the air as an inside-out person.

I'm not going to change my clothes today and I'm the material representation of an asshole that is six feet tall.

I don't know what time it is but I do know I'm not going to change my clothes today.

And I don't know what I'm doing.

You can borrow my socks if your feet are cold or if you just want to own something.

I'm not going to change my clothes today.

I SUCK

And maybe I get somewhere but my movement is decided by wanting to go, not wanting to go somewhere.

There are only small episodes where I can go without thinking about what I'm doing and how it is clearly not supposed to be like this. And that it will never end.

I have nervous rituals that only carry significance when I perform them alone. They are important to me.

Is it ok to sometimes see your own hands and jump back because you're worried someone is trying to choke you.

Guess what, it's too late, we're friends. And, something else, I can't remember.

And you will miss me, I know it. I know it.

HEY, MOLE ON THE LOWER BACK/UPPER ASSCHEEK OF THE GIRL STANDING IN FRONT OF ME AT THE POST OFFICE

Mole On The Lower Back/Upper Asscheek Of The Girl Standing In Front Of Me At The Post Office, how are you.

I want to marry you. Just you, Mole On The Lower Back/Upper Asscheek Of The Girl Standing In Front Of Me At The Post Office.

You are perfect.

Mole On The Lower Back/Upper Asscheek Of The Girl Standing In Front Of Me At The Post Office, do you need someone to look at you. I can do that. That's all I can do.

Make me a happy person. We are too right for each other to have to share. We shouldn't share.

I don't want many friends because I am too weak for that kind of work. I am too weak to have friends.

Mole On The Lower Back/Upper Asscheek Of The Girl Standing In Front Of Me At The Post Office, how are you—marry me, and I will break my fingers off using my bedroom door—make them into coins you can redeem for kisses.

And the kisses will make me weak.

Mole On The Lower Back/Upper Asscheek Of The Girl Standing In Front Of Me At The Post Office, stay with me.

NO TOLERANCE

I catch the flies on your corpse and take the blood back from each and rebuild you because I want to apologize for wasting the years you thought could've been used to do something even though I know you are wrong.

FOUR APOLOGIES

This is an apology to my roommate. You're right. I should've first asked you if you wanted an "artic adventure." And I should've explained that an "artic adventure" is when I dump a bunch of snow on you while you're sleeping. But we need to resolve this. Because someone needs to cook dinner for you and then not hear the words "thank you" even though they're so easy to say.

This is an apology to the comic book character on my underwear when I was five. I am sorry for shitting on a likeness of you when I was in kindergarten. I didn't know I had the flu. If I had known, I would've worn my striped underwear.

This is an apology to my bathroom floormat. I am sorry. I didn't know I'd become too destroyed to want to leave my apartment and wash you. If it's ok with you, I think I will fold you twice and then put you behind the toilet and forget about you.

This is an apology to the cat I saw smashed in the road. I couldn't remember how to perform cpr on a dead cat. Plus I didn't want to have to dodge cars.

HEY LEG-PINCHER, HOP ON MY BACK, I'M HORNY-NICE RIGHT NOW

We don't have anything in common.

FOR SOME THINGS, THERE IS NO ERASER

I can't help but think of how disgusted people must feel when I give them a hug.

And compliments are filth.

We should wash each other and suck the soap from the ends of each other's hair—put our hands in between the folds of each other's legs—hug to keep warm—and dry each other with gauze pulled from the skinny space that divides thinking something and saying something.

I am convinced that aside from my room, no other place exists.

But I'm not lost because I'm not looking to go anywhere.

I think about pushing everyone I meet.

Or making cookies for them and then coughing onto the cookies before I bring them over.

Or making my blood into ice cubes and mixing them a drink.

Or sometimes I don't think about anything and I just wait for the person to leave.

You get used-to things not working, but never the ways they stop working.

FEELING LIKE SHIT WAS AROUND BEFORE HUMAN BEINGS

Sometimes I put my hand in my pocket and find little stones and pieces of paper and I hold it all in my hand and say, "What happened to me" and I try to remember my multiplication tables to show that I am still a good person.

DON'T BE A DICK, LOVE ME

If you ever buy a pair of pants that have big enough pockets, please let me live with my head in your pocket.

I would be able to keep your leg warm with my laughing.

I would be able to tell you when your phone rings or whether or not you have enough change to buy certain things.

Get some pants that have big enough pockets please.

Sew them on if you have to I guess please.

At first it will be hard for you to walk with my head in your pocket, clinging to your leg.

But you will get used to it.

You will do anything for me I guess please.

Pull out your hair on a sleepwalk and stick it to the wall by the dead root ends I guess please.

Wait.

IT IS WEIRD TO BE AT A HOUSEPARTY WHERE EVERYONE IS ALIVE EXCEPT YOU

Every time I blink I'm worried everything else will die.

"Soft and shiny" is a good way to describe your hair after using some really good shampoo.

"Soft and shiny" is also a good way to describe a really old apple that is growing a beard of glitter.

Somebody just kill me already.

Email me and I'll give you my address and I'll leave my doors unlocked.

I'll even leave a big rock by my bed with a note by it that says, "Keep going, you're almost there!"

Yesterday, I put butter knives in my mouth and acted like a walrus. I wish someone was around to see it.

And the message is always the same.

I'm not trying to solve anything or help in any way.

The message is always the same.

FUCK YOU, DUMMY

My uvula is a birdcage trapping a scared, dying bird.

And loneliness is the reward for not wanting to contaminate someone else's life.

You can re-create the entire material world with a dot-to-dot.

Except for the paper where you diagram the dot-to-dot.

I BELIEVE IT'S OK TO PERMANENTLY DISFIGURE YOURSELF

Someone else usually says what I am thinking before I convince myself that no one else is thinking it or would ever think it.

I bought a small gift and wrapped it and hid it in my closet.

I found the small gift three months later and got really excited.

It was like someone cared about me.

It was like I convinced myself someone was thinking of me or would ever think of me.

Every day, I open the door to my closet and grab my coat then put on my coat and pause and think about getting into the closet and sitting down and shutting the door.

The only reason I don't do it sometimes is because I am worried I won't be able to find the doorknob again.

Things like that are scary.

And guess what, I'm fucking cool.

I recommend you treat the public like your own birthday party.

EVERYTHING IS A CALENDAR

Whenever I eat an apple I put the sticker on my shirt, and sometimes in the morning when I go to put on a shirt I notice a large collection of stickers and that's how I know how old I am. Yep.

AT A RESTAURANT I SAW A GUY WITH A LONG-ASS BEARD (NO, NOT LONG ASS-BEARD)

1. At a restaurant I saw a man with a very long beard. I said, "I like your beard." He said thanks. Then I said, "We should be friends."

2. At a restaurant I saw a man with a very long beard. I said, "I like your beard." He said thanks. Then I interlocked my fingers and put my thumbs together and said, "What do I have to do to walk away with that bad-boy in my pocket."

3. At a restaurant I saw a man with a very long beard. I said, "I like your beard." He said thanks. Then I said, "If I were riding you like a horse, I would hold onto you with both hands on either side of your beard." He said, "That's the only way to do it."

4. At a restaurant I saw a man with a very long beard. I said, "I like your beard." He said thanks. Then I said, "When it gets heavy with ideas, what do you do." He said, "I always shake it out before I enter my house." I nodded and said, "Ah."

5. At a restaurant I saw a man with a very long beard. I said, "I like your beard." He said thanks. Then I said, "If you're good today you can come over and I'll comb it and sing you a song." He said, "I'd like that."

6. Today at a restaurant I didn't talk to or look at anyone and I called myself boss.

IS VERY DIFFICULT TO UNDERSTAND WHAT OTHER PEOPLE THINK (IS VERY DIFFICULT)

Most of my day consists of attempting not to be noticed by people.

Sometimes when I notice someone looking at me, I say, "We can act like this never happened."

There is no afterlife. The afterlife is people taking turns telling you how stupid you are, without end.

I hate it when you put your arm over me while we're sleeping because it prevents me from getting up and running away as fast as I can.

Plus it makes me sweaty.

Plus I can't stop thinking about biting your arm really hard and seeing how long it takes you to wake up.

Plus you are a dead body.

Plus I hate being touched.

Plus I hate.

Priceless. Dying of cancer times a billion.

Is normal to never have fun. People who need to have fun

hate themselves and are afraid to die.

Is fun to wash my entire body with napkins. I wet with sink water then lie down on my couch feeling sorry for myself. Is very fun.

And now I will slowly breathe out the same air I was going to use to call myself a real motherfucker.

A real motherfucker is designed to produce real motherfuckers.

When you see someone you want to say hi to coming down the sidewalk, hide behind something then jump out and say hi.

Is very difficult not to become the entire world. Is very difficult.

Hi.

EARLIER I THOUGHT, "CUT A BIG WOUND INTO YOUR CHEST, IT'LL BE OK"

I found a turtle on the side of the street today. When I bent down to look, its head went into its shell. I said, "I know what you mean."

If I was a miniature farmer farming the carpet in my apartment, I would make a scythe out of a toenail clipping and a pretzel rod.

I don't know what I'm doing and I'm a dummy though.

And uh, the only way to bring something back to life is to leave it alone.

I wish there was a cord attached to my forehead that I could pull to raise my skull like a collapsible puppet.

What moves tree branches—is what sends a dead leaf out into the middle of a large puddle—is what pushes a flimsy moth into flight—is what in haphazard precision parts your hair—is what comes from where you can't see and calms your terror-face while you're trying to sleep—is what I eat and blow out into your face when I am on top of you or you are on top of me—is what will outlive us all—is nothing to be proud of.

This sucks.

A world of love would implode just as quickly as a world of hate.

Not everyone can be loved.

You are not important.

After I cut notches into your skeleton and climb to the top, I get to the top and feel cheated.

After I get to the top, I get to the top and I feel cheated and I will drop a rock and listen for it, to measure the height.

I WANT TO SCREAM IN SOMEONE'S FACE AND INTIMIDATE HIM/HER

It is the end when you don't want to trouble the only person who will still help you—when you are to them what you are to yourself.

It is the end when you are too stupid to move.

The tail of a dead animal in the street still moves because there is wind, not because it is still alive.

NEANDERTHAL CLITORIS

The worst position to be in is to have someone care about you more than you care about yourself.

The worst position to be in is to be that person.

The worst position is to be a person.

Everyone needs to hate someone else.

Being that someone else is as good a goal as any.

You are my favorite failure and I am too destroyed to get off the couch—I guess I'll sleep on the couch without brushing my teeth.

Everyone needs to hate being a sleepy failure with a goal but I want to be buried in a coffin—holding another human who died on the same day as me, both of us wearing crowns made of construction paper with plastic jewels glued on.

Ouch, this is hurting me.

Ouch.

The worst position is the one you began with and then continued to make worse.

I LIKE WHEN A GIRL HAS PAINTED NAILS/TOE-NAILS

The fly won't make it across the highway because there is so much wind and none of it moves in the same direction.

None of it moves in the same direction and nothing gets me hard anymore.

Some things are so pretty when I look at them I fear a stroke or some kind of instant death. Some things are so pretty I fucking hate them.

There is a part of me that intensely hates the sink in my bathroom. There is another part of me that thinks I just haven't gotten to know the sink in my bathroom well enough.

It will be easy to tape our hands to each other's heads, we just have to stay still.

It will be easy to get through this, we just have to stay still.

I am sitting on the sidewalk alone, brushing the sidewalk with an old leaf and I hope a plane falls on me.

Around the age of my death I won't remember today at all.

I have forgotten nearly everything that has ever happened to me.

The crumbs on my bed fill my mouth. I blow them up into my

ceiling fan and watch where they land. But I don't really care where they land because I will find them again and I will pick them all up again.

Involvement with other humans is difficult but sometimes people let you steal their better qualities if you can convince them those qualities are ugly.

And then um, you become a saint.

I DAYDREAM ABOUT MY HANDS BECOMING LIQUID

Money is stupid.

My mind is ruined.

Most peoples' parents make me intensely uncomfortable.

SILENT DINNERS FUCKING RULE

Don't wake up ever.

The indentation above you upper lip is my crib and I am never going to wake up and I won't be fun to find.

I drew a circle on the wall and I tell time by how my head moves through it as a shadow when I sit in front of it.

It is stupid that I have clothes and places to be and I think I have a wallet somewhere and a lot of cups around my room and that's it—I think that's all I have—but it's still pretty stupid.

Part of me wants to light my apartment on fire and just sit there.

Part of me wants to light my apartment on fire and run.

And when I wake up in the crib that is the indent above your upper lip I use the pieces of the crib to build a rocket to the top of your head.

Uh if I knew what your favorite color was I would make everything that color, including myself.

It is time to regret everything.

It is time to leave my arms in the sun so they soften and then stretch them long enough to be able to gently set you down far away.

I leave my arms in the sun and they soften and I stretch them, but now I can't touch anything that is directly in front of me.

It is best to think about nice things while I eat you clean of your period.

You lose.

A LOT OF PEOPLE LIVE IN CHICAGO (I'D SAY, A SHITLOAD)

Tonight I went out to get food and when I paid, I said to the woman, "Keep the pennies." She told me to have a nice night. I took the food and ate it in the snow, sitting next to a bush and a garbage can. I decided that I would squeeze the legs together of the next nice person I met and then refuse to let go until maybe that person tried to attack me. I went to sip my drink but there was no straw in place. I looked for a straw but there was no straw. I decided the next nice person I encountered I'd pin down and appreciate. Sometimes I'm ruined.

I HAVE BAD URGES

There is no way to teach someone how to gently take apart a human life when that someone is the someone who taught you.

It is impossible not to want to do certain things.

And I saved everyone some time by feeling as unhappy as I could, unassisted.

I don't like it when the water gets cold around my ankles in the shower. I usually think, "Oh shit" and I look up at the ceiling like there might somehow be an escape.

You are my favorite person in the whole wide world though.

And I like myself. And I like you.

There is nothing you can do to kill me, so don't even touch me at all it makes me hate you that you think that's even possible.

My sex organs ache, always.

TWO PEOPLE KICKING MY HEAD AT THE SAME TIME, ONE IN FRONT AND ONE BEHIND

I cut my lips up into little flaps and then run them over your face and say, "Stay still, this is called 'Painting the House I Will Never Own' and it will never be over."

Then I repeat the phrase, "It will never be over" while continuing to paint the house I will never own.

The bigger the hearts get the more my teeth scrape them when I put them into my mouth but I will force them down whole, I promise that.

Swallow them whole and feel them pass through my organs, slowly each.

It will never be over.

You deserve a long afterlife that consists of a single hug from someone whose face you never see.

And you deserve to push me out a window while I am talking about how pretty it is outside. Be like, "Why don't you get a better look" and then push me out the window. Or suggest my shoe is untied, then do it.

I am worried I can't do it myself.

I HAVE A BIG BUTT

When people are storms, stand under them.

And use them to help you grow plants that look pretty and smell pretty but bear little needles filled with poison—because they will only touch you when you're attractive and you'll only touch them when you know it will hurt.

Keep your eyes open on other people.

Hate other people.

WHEN I GO FOR WALKS I PURPOSELY BRUSH UP AGAINST BUSHES AND STREET SIGNS BECAUSE, I DON'T KNOW, IT JUST FEELS SO RIGHT

Your bloody crawl is a red carpet.

Popped cherry is lipstick.

And somehow your bedroom floor is my grave.

I am horny to be a dead bird, smashed in a drinking fountain at the park.

Make me feel uncomfortable about saying anything—this can be done by saying nothing.

I don't know what I'm doing.

Our hymen hangs flimsy with holes from hungry insects.

I eat our hymen with little zipper teeth.

The zipper teeth spread my gumlines and my attempts not to smile are disgusting.

Our hymen is my bathing suit—make me a pool with what you wring out of your pretty long hair.

Our hymen is a cloth I wave to assert allegiance, not block the heat.

When we go on a picnic I spread your part of the blanket over a fire.

All pulses are such bullshit.

I am almost done.

Take yourself out of the best friend game without saying goodbye.

By not saying hi.

DON'T BE A STEREOTYPE
(OR DO, I DON'T CARE)

I have made many mistakes, but I'm not upset.

Between the ground and the air there is a plane of pure indifference that is exactly as tall as me.

Underneath my feet is becoming soft.

I would like it if I was a centimeter tall, unknown to everyone.

First thing I'd do is lie down in the carpet and sleep for a whole day straight.

Look out, here comes 2:53 a.m. and I don't have a family resemblance to anything but the combined sounds all animals make to alert when they're hurt.

I must be a hundred miles tall because when I lie down and then get up I feel far from where I began—same thing when I lie down.

There is only one lesson. There is only one lesson.

If I figured out what I was doing, I'd stop doing it.

Some things explode without moving.

Show yourself how to explode without moving.

Awesome.

There is only one kind of hurt and it comes to you in varying degrees of prevalence and uh, the worst degree feels like nothing is happening at all.

Holy fucking shit.

Forever is an idea that people made up to feel sorry for themselves.

Get on with becoming tired.

Be a stereotype then jump out of hiding when people have forgotten you exist.

Get on with becoming a tired stereotype.

There are many ways to say what seems like a lie but is completely true.

You can't teach yourself how to play on a playground when there is no one else there.

And you can't learn anything when there are other people there.

REALLY BIG CARROT

I bought a really big carrot at the store and I sat on a bench at the park eating the really big carrot and there was a kid doing somersaults. He was wearing a watch that looked cool. I thought about telling him how cool his watch looked but he seemed busy. I thought, "He will never know how I feel about his watch." He said, "That's a really big carrot" and I nodded and he somersaulted away. He looked really dizzy. I bet I could've easily pushed him over. Let's see, what else.

PASSIVE DEATH ALL DAY LONG

It's weird how many people I don't know.

I enjoy taking my life for granted—if you're asking me to do that with you, then yes I will. Then yes.

Cut out a circle of black construction paper and yell into it when you're scared.

And call me a name only you know.

I bury you in a grave of red light.

And everyone in heaven is homeless.

There are some things that I actually know.

I know I want to come on your face from really far away.

And I know I don't feel bad when someone blames me for making a mistake.

If I had a mascot, it would be an unidentified dead body with some dirt on its face and one of its pockets turned inside out and maybe both arms mangled, wearing a fanny pack that is full of dried bruises, and a dented face with a ripped-eyelid not covering the eye anymore.

Or maybe my mascot would be a hair that fell to the ground and blew beneath the closet door.

Or maybe I don't know.

I don't know how to look at anything the right way.

It is difficult to find something to look at when you don't want to look at anything.

Oh yeah, I just want to pinch you until you cry.

And nothing is clean enough to touch me.

I enjoy taking my life for granted and if you are asking to do that with me, then yes.

Yes I will.

So set my skinny corpse on a swing at a playground and never talk to me again, like you want to.

Set my skinny corpse on a swing at the playground and leave it there and walk away.

Last night I stood in the drive-thru of a restaurant and stared at the camera and smiled and waved. I kept doing that until an employee came out. Then I ran. I hid behind a bush in the parking lot of a bank and rubbed my fingers in the mulch and smelled them and I didn't want to leave.

UNTITLED

Behind every face is an expressionless skull.

This is true about anybody.

I can't tell if I'm really interested in anything.

And look, I didn't know that if I grabbed your face while you were sleeping and tried that thing where you pull a tablecloth off a table without disturbing what's on top, that it would hurt that much. I'm just an idiot human.

Glue a knife to your tongue and lick my belly like a bitch.

THE NAP (PART 2)

This morning I realized I was eager for the mailman to come (so I could see another person (even though I am almost convinced my mailman hates me and is secretly planning to kill me (pretty sure she wants to steal my blood and take my blood away in a bag then throw the bag into a big hole and bury it (pretty sure I am going to take a nap this afternoon (pretty sure I hate life because it is one long nap that breaks in intervals of waking up to being a completely different person, never achieving any result because never feeling exactly the same))))).

This line right here is one I put in as a way to make a pause, and feel calm again, hope that's ok with you.

A CERTAIN AMOUNT OF SEX ACTUALLY FEELS BAD

With a piece of sidewalk nailed behind my face, I'd still find a way to lift my face.

With a piece of sidewalk nailed behind my face, nothing would change.

I'd still lift my face and keep it off the ground.

I'd still change nothing.

With two lives I'd use the first to figure out how to make the next one even worse.

Do you believe me.

We can meet in the corner of space where people forget to check—where I do things I have to do with my eyes closed.

The fifth orgasm rips the groin the bestest and I am a beautiful human.

I eat jewelry and give nothing in return.

And youth is the thing that keeps ending.

Unlikely future.

No one has to protect the animal with the big jaw from the

cross-eyed palsy holding a bb gun.

The cross-eyed palsy holding a bb gun threatens nothing.

The ground will get cold soon and I'm waiting to be there, to freeze with it and be cold until the sun tries its best to get beneath and cook me.

I actually feel ill with how negative I have become.

But I don't have any negative feelings about the carpet in my apartment.

And I don't have any positive feelings about cleaning it.

I only have interest in continuing to rub my feet on it then sending electricity through my nose to my cat's nose to give my cat braindamage (hopefully (wink wink)).

All things keep ending.

Do you believe me.

YOU WILL NOT CELEBRATE

When you know all the words to some television commercials you will not celebrate.

GROSS BODY GETTING FED THROUGH A PINCHED-OPEN MOUTH

When I take my temperature it reads: "Fucking perfect."

Please take good care of my frozen ghost. Don't let it look at the sun.

Today a car drove by me and someone yelled, "Fucking human."

That face-down-on-the-couch-you-wouldn't-get-up-if-the-ghost-of-the-previous-decade-called-from-the-hallway kind of tired. That kind. You know.

God bless America. There is so much of my semen on your bedspread you will never forget me.

I am having hurt insides all the time. But that doesn't matter.

I am convinced I don't have actual organs.

There are only bags of water inside me.

Winners are always violent.

Winners are always looking for more losers, because people only lose once.

Maybe I am full of shit.

Yes, I am full of shit.

But sometimes I accidentally tell the truth.

And everything kills everything else.

I wish there was a really small room in your house that I could live in and never leave. I'd get thinner and thinner but never die. You'd check every once in a while to see if I was still there and every time I'd say, "hi" and probably nothing else.

Everything else.

GETTING SHOT IN THE EYE WITH AN ARROW PROBABLY WON'T EVER HAPPEN TO ME (FINGERS CROSSED)

The ideal place at someone else's house is kneeling with your face stuck between the cushions of a couch.

I am most afraid of forgetting how to do things and then being embarrassed when I can't do them in front of others like I said I could.

It is impossible to inhale water without hurting your chest.

Maybe I am floating above a tree that is on fire, breathing in the smoke and maybe I like who you are but it is difficult to figure out what to do with my hands when a lot of people are looking.

There are little rocks in my urethra and I paint each one with a nontoxic marker and fill a cartridge with them then shoot myself in the chest and call it a constellation.

The whole world shares the same memory bank.

Forgive the people who would die without your forgiveness but do it right after they have almost died.

UNTITLED II

I wonder if doctors that deliver babies ever do a trick similar to that "quarter in your ear" trick except with like, a nerf football soaked in fake-blood. Everything I do is proof I didn't do the thing before it well enough. Get over this. You can do it.

THE LAST TIME I SAID SOMETHING RACIST, IT WAS UNINTENTIONAL, I WAS IN SECOND GRADE AND I MADE MY (FIRST) MEXICAN GIRLFRIEND CRY AND IT SUCKED

A sleeping bag at the bottom of a lake is my preferred afterlife just so you know in case you're in charge.

Today after you leave I nail boards over the door.

If you try to come back before I have the boards all the way nailed up then I nail you to the wall and walk away and never come back.

I can solve anything.

We can halt our debts if you just admit I am better than everyone else, at everything else.

I SAW FLIES ALL OVER MY ROOM LAST NIGHT AND I WASN'T ON DRUGS

There is no name for the color of your cheeks when you are hurt and halfdead and wishing you could float away, eyes closed.

There is nothing prettier than the color of your cheeks when you are too hurt to speak, wishing I'd float away, eyes closed.

There is no way I will ever float away because I am too heavy right where I am and there is no way you will float away because I am your orbit.

Yeah I'm your orbit.

Ugly girls make me harder than pretty girls yeah.

And yeah I have on a sweater that needs to be washed yep.

I feel good because I stopped trying to be a human yep.

I had sex two nights ago but I am so alone yep.

I can make anyone's life better than my own by simply staying away.

Lightbulbs holding different colored ink make my body cavity move and I hope they don't break I guess yep.

When your cold hand is under my shirt on my back I am even

less human than usual.

That should hurt your feelings.

When I come in my sleep uh the whole world is deflowered.

I go to the bathroom and wash my hands clean of the smell of your hair and then I am weightless.

That should hurt your feelings.

My self-tracing daydreams remind me of myself ouch.

That should hurt my feelings.

I feel like something ended a long time ago and I can't figure out what happened but I know it's important.

My life will end prematurely yep.

I forget a lot of people without even trying.

That should hurt feelings.

There is no name for that color, but I think about it as I'm floating away halfdead, eyes-closed.

SOME PEOPLE DESERVE TO BE TREATED POORLY

I like to know when a kiss is coming; I don't like to be surprised.

I identify with pieces of spiral notebook paper that get ripped out but, like, split down the side all crappily.

The transformation from sleepy to more sleepy is always, and I am only good at getting thrown into bigger piles of things that don't work.

You can always change my mind though.

And I can always get along with anyone.

Some people deserve to be treated poorly though.

They will announce themselves though.

CRUSHING IRRITATION
(OUTSIDE I FEEL UGLY)

A grave for a string is a straight line.

A grave for anything else is the shape of that anything else.

There is nothing wrong with being a fucking failure.

It takes more than one person to make a fucking failure.

I want to thread my face with wire and hang from my face until I pass out.

There will never be new sounds.

I can't imagine the task of remaining completely still.

I teach a space how much it holds by filling it.

I invented the colors and lines that make up a confused face.

Not going to fail at anything ever—that's how I feel.

And the purest moment of panic is when everything is right.

I wouldn't be surprised if I put my hand on the back of my head and it just went through my face without feeling anything and uh yes your ghost lives off the sweat from my sleeping forehead, so there.

You can bother others by just sitting still.

And yes a grave for a human is a skull.

And yes I will start an orphanage by abandoning myself.

My eulogy will be "sometimes nice but sometimes an asshole" or "sometimes had feelings" or "always shared" or "always worried about things that never happened."

THE GUM ON THE FLOOR IS ME
(IS ME ON THE FLOOR)

Last night I was ordering a sandwich and the employee asked me if I wanted the sandwich toasted. I pointed my finger at the employee's face and said, "One day, everything will be toasted, and you will be the first, sweetheart." When I filled my fountain drink, the flavor was empty; it was just seltzer water. I took one sip and set the drink down and walked away. I walked away thinking, "There is nowhere far enough to walk."

THE APOCALYPSE HAPPENS EVERY TIME SOMEONE DIES

The worst part about being alive is thinking about it.

I farm gravedirt.

Today I was sitting in a chair at a restaurant eating and I felt a little hand on my head and I turned around and there was a woman holding a baby and the woman said, "He just wants to touch your head" and I said, "That's fine" and then the baby laughed and slapped my head a little bit.

I wish I were my girlfriend because then I wouldn't exist or at least I could act like I didn't.

Is hard not to feel like my bed is a lake when you're so sleepy and blue-faced and heavy. Is hard.

I am hard right now and I smell terrible.

What's new with you.

Everyone is describing the same thing.

I am part of the thing being described.

Another part of the thing described is everyone describing it.

I want to break someone's jaw with my head. For real.

I think maybe I forgot to say hello at the beginning of this.

I'm real sorry.

WE ARE GOOD AT BECOMING OLDER

Being insecure is the best way to protect what you no longer want.

And every day I remember things that remind me I'm a brand new human every few seconds and every few seconds I'm reminded I'm always a brand new version of the same person—never different—reinvented every few seconds as the same aging pile of ridiculous garbage.

I am ok with that.

God bless my shapeless head.

At night my head deforms into dragonflies that collide with trees and eat their own wings to stay alive.

Real life is a low-moving wind in the shape of a scythe.

I am ok with that.

And everyone I meet loves me.

I win over so many hearts I need a bigger chest.

The best way to get older is to try not to.

So be happy.

Because I'm willing to build a treehouse in your backyard to protect you.

Can I come over and sit in your fridge.

What time will you come over and hammer me into the ground with your balled hand.

Fuck my birthday, but yeah.

No one trusts you if you think no one trusts you.

I HOPE I GIVE A CONVINCING THANK YOU TO SOMEONE BEFORE I DIE

There will always be something I can't tell someone else.
And there will always be someone else who doesn't want to listen.

Sometimes I'm convinced that everything and everyone is an arrangement meant only for me to experience and that an afterlife is not something you bridge but experience through unending life.

And when you are surrounded by people who care about you, you will never hit the ground and that's a bad thing I guess, so what.

I have never heard a person say, "so what" unconvincingly.

I want to offer help to someone with his/her groceries then throw the groceries on the ground and bend myself into a crab-like stance, hissing at the person to make him/her think I feel threatened.

I own everything.

I can't believe I own everything.

A pie chart of the percentage of my time spent worrying would be a monochromatic circle and I'd be able to draw it with my eyes closed.

If you move from worse to worse you will always have just been better.

It'd be nice to just knock on someone's door and hand them an apple. "Thought you might need this, you know, for whatever." Then smile and walk away, not looking back.

When I haven't clipped my toenails in a long time I get paranoid someone else will see them and accuse me of being an animal.

I wouldn't mind being killed and stuffed like an animal, but I would mind being treated like an animal you just hit with a shoe to expel from somewhere.

If someone hits me with his/her shoe, I would feel worthless.

So bad being the person that is this particular amount of experiences, thought about and remembered this particular way.

But there is no way to know whether or not I am jealous of anyone else.

Worried about trying to befriend everyone you meet, you be the shittiest person ever, sure.

Call me when you have some time.

BOO

Boo—I think you'll love rubbing our bellybuttons together to make them whistle.

Boo—I think you'll love trying this new thing.

Boo—I'll wear a paperbag over my head if you stab me repeatedly in the chest.

Boo—I'm going to handcuff you to yourself at seven years old.

Boo—I'm almost entirely convinced no one really likes me.

WHERE DOES GLITTER COME FROM, IS THERE LIKE, A MINE?

After I remove my nervous system, I stretch it over my lap and poke it repeatedly with a needle that I have not cleaned, the whole time singing a song that reverses my age.

And uh, you are always alone.

And for as many people as there are, it feels like there is only me.

At night I sit in a folding chair in my room.

Sometimes I just sit naked and look out the window.

I think about running and tripping face-first through the window.

If someone hugged me right now, the world would be solved.

Everything should be how I want it but I don't really care.

I just exploded and returned to form in one of tonight's many silences.

COPS FREAK ME OUT BECAUSE I DON'T LIKE WHEN PEOPLE TRY TO CONTROL ME

If you don't hate yourself, everybody else will.

And they will never do as good a job.

There is no one I wouldn't watch, to learn a new way.

You are my favorite though. You are the very best work.

26 years ago I was born when a waterlogged tree split in two and I stepped out exactly how I am now, 26 years old, already declining in new and wonderful ways.

ELDERLY COUPLE

Tonight I sat in a booth at a fast food restaurant and looked out the window and in the parking lot there was an elderly couple sitting in their car eating ice cream together and they looked so happy that I asked one of the employees to kill them for me but instead of complying, the employee asked me to leave. I waved to the elderly couple in the parking lot as I walked by. It's hard not to become an elderly couple yourself when the only person you talk to is yourself and you're so in love.

CAT SKULL

I like to put my hand beneath my pillow then pull it out, act like it's a surprise gift.

Frowns need friends too.

I guess I am the shittiest human ever, I guess.

I have become paranoid that people are mailing me nice letters saying how much they want to touch me and kiss me and comb my hair but the mailman is throwing the letters out just to cause pain in my life.

There are no new ways to make an enemy.

And no new ways to give a gift.

How are you going to leave.

Me, I plan on standing still and letting it pass, never acknowledging that what is hurting me is hurting me.

I WORSHIP SATAN

I'll breathe on the windows and trace a face that is mine and yours.

I'll rip your ear open with a secret.

The secret will turn to icicles stringing the torn canal.

Say hurray for the length of time you get to make things happen.

Say hurray, you fucking ingrate.

If you come to my apartment I will let you drink some of my blood and you won't even have to pay for it.

When we go on a picnic together I spread your part of the blanket over a hole that leads to the opposite side of the planet.

When I was rereading this, I saw the words "blanket" and "planet" and that made me think of a planet whose surface is all blankets.

And I loved the planet.

Hail satan!

He is good!

SELF-ESTEEM

I'm combing your hair with my fingers, you motherfuckers. And yep, the receipt for my kisses is a leaf stapled to your cheek and you feel blessed. Don't worry, I will not refuse to offer you a hammock in my heartvalve when you look really tired. And yep, I love myself. I get blisters in my throat from holding in all the nice things I want to tell myself. I love myself and yep I love my throat blisters, they are the receipts for the kisses I get from people I don't trust and it's hard not to become tired when everyone is the same.

HOLOGRAPHIC PERSONALITY DISGRACE

I'm only mean to you because I have a crush on you.

I'm not trying to hurt anyone's feelings uh I wish I could cup my hands around the blackest corner of my closet and bring it to you and say, "See this, do you understand."

Turn around real quick, you'll see the thing that was following you and you'll regret what it is but not that you saw it.

Sometimes I have to go to the bathroom or a private place when I'm in public so I can clench both of my fists and grind my teeth and kneel down and press my face against the ground until the energy goes away.

The energy is not my best friend.

I'm in a canoe inside one of your veins and when I get to your heart I am going to stretch out and then do a cartwheel and laugh loudly until all the laughs start ricocheting and I have to be careful I don't get caught in my own barrage.

Or some-shit.

Some people are just assholes.

Some people are such assholes that saying, "Look, again, I'm sorry I cut off my thumb and glued it to your baby's head because I thought you'd like him better as a unicorn" means nothing to them.

Some people are assholes.

And everyone must have a crush on me because I feel like shit.

RELATIONSHIP

I am waiting for you to make a mistake.

And I am certain you die in my lap, in that you are a matchstick on a glacier.

Forget the very small attempts to boost your esteem that have been made by people all your life because I am staring at your forehead and it owes me some time alone and I owe it a hole for the world to step in and clean their feet off before saying hi and staying over way too long.

ONE THING CAN EXPLAIN EVERYTHING ELSE

The sunshine left inside the skin gets microwaved out.

Blood cells left inside the muscle get made into perfume and make-up for our faces.

The frisbee upside down still holding very cold rain gets tipped over to prevent small animals from drinking.

The muscles that make our genitals get unwound and thrown upward and when they fall on our faces we laugh and thank the sky for deciding not to kill us just yet because we have so many more important things to do.

The things around us get made into things we want to have and we are the things around us.

I ALWAYS THINK, "IF I JUST GET A GOOD AMOUNT OF SLEEP I'LL BE FINE"

But I never seem to get the right amount of sleep.

Last night I came in my sleep, sleeping on my back with both arms pinned, and when I woke up, my room was a giant black cube funneling itself into my mouth and nose and I was afraid and I couldn't move my arms.

One day I will fulfill my greatest aspiration when I walk down the sidewalk and take off my pants and beneath the pants there will be another pair of pants and then I keep walking, never returning to retrieve the previous pair of pants.

And no one is going to cry when I'm dead.

I AVOID WASHING DISHES BECAUSE I USUALLY REMEMBER SOMETHING AWFUL IN THE SILENCE

The best position to be in is sitting on the couch with nowhere to be—or no, facedown on the couch with nowhere to be.

I wouldn't mind living another eighty years if I never had to see anyone again.

Or if someone mandated that I had to wash a stack of dishes that took me eighty years to finish.

The best position to be in is not knowing what the best position is.

LITTLE KIDS AND ANIMALS LIKE ME

I bought some sidewalk chalk and then I drew a person on the street and I feel asleep next to it—facing it—so I'd be the first thing it saw upon waking up, like I was the best thing ever (which I am).

I shaved off pieces of your heart and wallpapered my room with them.

And my head falls to pieces, which become headstones for the things I say I will do tomorrow.

PLEASE ADOPT ME

It should be illegal to look at another person without his/her permission.

My superpower is that I am a fucking asshole and I can't remember anything.

My superpower is that I only remember things that benefit me.

I want to sneak into your room and cut your mattress open and get inside your mattress so that only my face is showing.

Won't that be fun.

My face will be under your covers.

We can be friends and I can entertain you, to avoid feeling like a chore.

We can work out a system of bites and licks so if you ever roll over on me while you're sleeping, I can communicate that I am dying or that I just need to talk.

I wish cereal still made me excited.

Kill people by ignoring them.

And please please please, don't litter.

I LIKE TO HURT OTHER PEOPLES' FEELINGS SOMETIMES (I MEAN SOMETIMES IT ACTUALLY FEELS LIKE THE ONLY SKILL I POSSESS ABOVE ALL OTHERS)

When I wake up, I smell the clothes on my floor and whichever smells most like me I wear—otherwise I feel upset the whole day.

Just kidding, I always feel upset.

Just kidding, I'm good.

The number of shapes you can imagine in the atmosphere is infinite based on how small you imagine them and how long you keep trying.

Trying hard is the first step to being upset and not trying anything else for a while.

And getting to know something or someone is the first step towards harming it.

And someone will search my room hard for the remains of my shape.

Touchdown for me, you rat-bastards.

If life is a gift it's best to reject the gift, and not be greedy.

SELF-INFLICTED CONTRACEPTIVE IDEA

We fill a plastic shopping bag with dead bugs and study them in the bathtub.

And I admit that sometimes right after I wake up I stand on my bed and try to jump my head into the ceiling so my neck breaks.

Sometimes when you're not looking I take your shoes away from the front door and hide them so you think you have disappeared. And that is half true.

Sometimes I wear my shoes while I am sleeping because I'm worried the bad people will try to cut my toes off.

I like to sleep with pants on too so I can keep my hands in my pockets and feel safe.

If your jawbone fell off and mine did too, we could sleep upside down with our top teeth clenched. And it would be nice.

The window in my room is either what brings the entire world into my room or the thing that keeps the entire world out. And that is half true.

I never make a mistake.

Nobody is different and I think we should just agree to be the most important people in each others' lives because why not.

Every time I look at myself in the mirror on my showerdoor I look exactly the same. I always look so tired.

And since nobody is different, I am the most important person in my life.

And I never make a mistake.

COMMIT CRIMES/
KILL YOUR PARENTS/
LIGHT SOMETHING ON FIRE/
STEAL SOMETHING

Most of my day consists of attempting not to be noticed by other people.

Sometimes that involves jumping into bushes, or hiding beneath cars.

Sometimes that involves just smiling at someone.

It would require the biggest vacuum ever to take away my greatness.

So don't touch me.

Randomly asking someone if they are frightened is a good way to frighten them.

I like to take out a cellphone in public and pretend someone is on the other line. I like to say, "You bet your ass I want to dig out your tongue and suck the blood out of your screaming mouth, when are you available."

People are impressed when it seems like you have things to do.

The times I wake up and see a hair on my pillow, I think maybe you came over and lay down for a while and left, but usually it's just a stray armpit hair of mine—which makes me think about what you'd look like with a head full of armpit hairs—which makes me think I would like you so much more if all the hair on your head was armpit hair.

And things end when not given attention.

Be very upset when things end.

Be happy that things end.

Commit the greatest crimes by letting yourself end.

IDEALLY AT SOME POINT IN MY LIFE I'D LIKE TO EMERGE FROM AN ALLEY AND STAND IN FRONT OF PEOPLE ON THE STREET AND SAY, "REAL PAIN" WITHOUT LOOKING AT ANY OF THEM, THEN RETREAT BACK INTO THE ALLEY

People die.

Don't worry, people die.

Sometimes when I'm wiping my ass, I look at the toilet paper with the shit on it and I say, "People die" but I mean it more as an assurance.

You must be a mouse because I always find you frozen and scared on the kitchen floor.

You must be my best friend because it seems like you never existed.

We should buy an extra big pair of jeans and get into them together and do a cartwheel.

I am the only furniture in my apartment and vague disappointment is the only furniture in me.

I am the only furniture in my apartment and big disappointment is the only furniture in me.

FALLING ASLEEP ON THE COUCH = FAILURE

I wear gloves in the shower to make sure I don't accidentally touch myself.

Don't teach anything, except how to be a seizure of space.

I lick the cold water along the bottom of the kitchen sink when it's really late and I don't know what to do or if there is even anything to do.

Is easy to feel like my only option is to pull my hood over my head and duct-tape it shut and then roll around on the floor screaming.

Is very easy.

I don't recognize myself when I am talking to someone.

Myself, the only human alive.

My headstone will be a mirror.

The distance from me to another human is making my legs wobble.

But there is nothing I can do.

There is nothing to do but hide.

I want to be a vampire that only drinks blood out of your hip.

I will be a nice enough vampire to only drink enough blood each night to survive.

I won't like, go all out or anything, and totally kill you.

Because then I'd have to find a new person and a new hip and we have such a good relationship going anyway.

My superpower is that I can't deal with everyday situations without feeling like that last bit of semen that clogs my pisshole after I'm done fucking myself.

Uh, fuck yeah.

Is very easy.

I would be in a commercial for apple juice if someone asked me.

I hope that you live a long life of many nice moments, until you die, staring at the ceiling with the swaying light of the blinds projected, less nice than the sun but still very nice like something you might want to jump into.

No one needs to have their feelings hurt. No one deserves anything.

I hope we live to be a hundred so it takes us a hundred years to die. Is very easy.

PEOPLE WHO DO COCAINE ARE USUALLY FUCKHEAD DICK CULTURE

The back of my forehead feels very dirty.

THERE IS NO WAY TO WASTE TIME

The wires that control my mouth feel thin.

It has become hard to say things that make people nod.

Some people will only welcome you back when you are injured badly.

And what is sharp is mine to use.

I expect the same of you.

Clean the tools from yesterday.

Reach into the air and pull down your weapon and use it on me.

What is sharp I expect you to clean and use on me.

Make your pillow a small lake.

Make your teeth twenty-eight weapons.

Make your way to hell.

Make the earth shed the layers you step on, out of embarrassment at having your marks on its skin.

OXYGEN IS PRETTY GOOD

I don't have to accept anything about anyone.

And I feel like I am stupid looking when I smile.

If I could tape myself to your ceiling to become part of your life without you knowing it, I would.

If I could cut my tongue out and hide it in your room, I would.

If I could do a backflip, I would start a campfire and do a backflip into the campfire and try to just lay there.

Useless-pile type of gone.

If I could maintain lasting relationships with other humans and not feel like I was slowly getting my head ripped off by an invisible cloud, then I would probably maintain lasting relationships with other humans.

Useless-head type of gone.

Fog on, brother.

If I could tape myself to your ceiling and secretly become part of your life, I would leave my socks inside my shoes beneath me and then when you look up, I'd say, "You are so great it exploded me out of my shoes and now I am stuck on your ceiling, can I please stay."

But I'm at a point now where I honestly think I don't try at all to get people to like me, and it feels weird.

I DARE YOU NOT TO DIE WHEN I LICK THE BOTTOM OF YOUR FOOT WHILE WE'RE FUCKING

The thing about when someone dies is, they never expect anything from you again and you don't expect anything from them either.

That's the thing.

I hope I am not remembered by anyone.

Not having hope is not the same as being hopeless.

You're having fun, but it will end.

WHEN I MAKE A PEANUT BUTTER SANDWICH AND LOOK AT MY REFLECTION ON THE MICROWAVE I LAUGH AND SAY, "YOU SILLY MAN" THEN I EAT THE SANDWICH ALONE IN THE KITCHEN, LEANING MY BACK AGAINST THE COUNTERTOP

Me and you as small-enough to float on our backs in a puddle.

(Me and you hoping that the puddle is close enough to space to freeze)

Me and you shooting each other in the face at the exact same time.

(Me and you hoping we hit the ground at the same time, next to each other)

Me and you rubbing our assholes together.

(Me and you remaining good friends)

Me and you as a single body with two heads weighing down a struggling spine ready to peel.

(Me and you knowing we're too pretty for the stem)

Me and you with our backs broken, lying on the carpet in the living room not able to think of anything to say or even actual words.

(Me and you knowing we're the same thing)

Me and you being quiet

(Me and you and nothing else)

My high-fives turn arms to shreds.

And I don't feel embarrassed by anything anymore.

Right now I could get shot in the chest and stomach many times and not die.

Yowzers!

IN SIXTH GRADE I WATCHED THE JANITOR BEAT MY CLASSMATE AND I LAUGHED (OH HOW I LAUGHED)

A telemarketer called me today and I said, "Please don't hang up on me, please."

I can be confused for a napkin—skipping a playground at night—caught by a cold puddle and made too heavy to fly.

When you die I am going to use your body as a sleeping bag.

I rim my thoughts with gold and let them drop dead at the front of my mind before I say them—that's why I smile a lot.

I just want one friend whose sole job is to remember things I am likely to forget.

I pulled a scab off my knee and fed it to a bird.

And everyone loves me.

Cover the earth in mirrors and redirect the sun. And space melts in black streams and I open my mouth to each stream.

Each stream collects in deposits in my organs and makes my body fail.

I place myself in a drainage canal, lying down, completely still, without any emotion.

And you will not forgive me because I won't ask.

There is a pimple on my upper cheek, under my right eye, and it fucking hurts.

I cut down my family tree. I pulled up the trunk and broke each root in half. Laughter was the soundtrack. And tonight I will start a bonfire with the timber and stare at it until it answers my questions. I will put my head in the bonfire and keep my eyes open until they melt. Then I will put a small crab in each socket and hunt down all my idols with a saw in my hand.

Stay alive by not smiling, or, go fuck yourself.

I can be confused for my own ideal sex mate.

And everyone loves me.

COMPLEX NEUROTIC VISIONARY TORTURE

You are gum because you are useless after a few seconds and because when I take you out of my mouth and throw you into the street you get eaten by birds and it makes me laugh and I never think about you again. I think you could say the same about me.

"ASSWIPE" IS A GOOD WAY TO DESCRIBE SOME PEOPLE, OR MAYBE I AM WRONG

I saw my face in a puddle today. Then a twig fell from a tree and ruined the whole thing. When the puddle reformed, I saw my face again and thought, "Is that right."

Tic-tac-toe—I win every time because I always occupy the middle.

Tic-tac-toe—I am always in the middle.

Look how small my heart is.

I am a bug—am a rolled up newspaper.

I steal the wings off other bugs and throw the wings into the garbage.

And I wake up laughing a lot.

Sometimes I feel like my life is very empty and sometimes it feels too full to survive.

But I lose every time because there is no middle.

I DON'T WEAR TURTLE-NECK SHIRTS BECAUSE OF THE POWERLESS TERROR I EXPERIENCE WHEN MY HEAD GETS STUCK

The good thing about living in a tree is that you get no visitors.

At night I put my hand beneath a rock. I keep my hand cold underneath a rock all night and by morning you are the rock and your ass is my nylon mask and I am breathing eggs into you, and you say, "You destroyer you."

I wouldn't want to be a melting ice cube because I'd be afraid of not knowing where I was going.

Get no visitors.

Get home without looking at anyone.

There are folds in my skin that shake out the smoke from everything old and burnt.

I don't blame myself for falling asleep in one of the folds and giving up—because I'm old and burnt.

I don't blame myself for falling asleep.

And nobody belongs anywhere until they are old and burnt.

Until they get no visitors.

Until they get home without looking at anyone.

PAINLESS, WELL-WISHER EXTINCTION

I take big bites out of the sun and feel it expand in me.

And all feelings get eaten, and become stone, because they are small and worthless.

But they never erode, and today is the day I lie down on the floor and let the stones expand through my chest, snapping ribs upward into buildings that take big bites out of the sun.

I'M CONFUSED WHEN PEOPLE ASK, "WHAT ARE YOU GOING TO DO TODAY."

Hiding behind the bathroom door is one way to make your roommate uncomfortable (email me if you want the rest of the ways)

Filling a glove with blood and putting it in the freezer is one way to make a blood-hand popsicle (email me if you want the rest of the ways)

I get scared about dying when I remember that dying means you can't change anything anymore. But I can't even do that now so whatever. I will keep breathing until I try to breathe and I can't, and I just think, "This is ok."

SLOWLY NEGLECTING A RELATIONSHIP

Eternity in a combination-safe on the top of a mountain.

Uh huh.

Whenever someone says, "There are plenty of fish in the sea," I think, "There are many ways to boil the sea."

As a human, I am worthless.

As a thing that is quiet, I am best.

As a friend, I am both.

As the person who taped you to the bed last night because I was afraid you'd get away, I'm guilty.

As a person right now, I am hoping that someone poisoned the toast I made for breakfast and I just don't know about it yet but that it will kill me and put me to sleep on the floor of my bedroom underneath the ceiling fan, the one with the missing lightbulbs.

Fuck yeah, I feel better.

THERE IS NOTHING TO DO

Very unfair that I'm a human and not a stick.

HAVING A CELLPHONE MAKES ME FEEL CORNERED BUT I COULD SAY THE SAME THING ABOUT HAVING EYES TOO, I THINK

One time I fell off my bed while I was sleeping and hit my mouth on the ground and in the morning I woke up back in bed with my bloody lips stuck to the pillow.

It was bad having to pull my bloody lips off the pillow.

Something else, but I forgot.

And all I can do is shrug.

I stand in the corner of my room leaning my weight against my forehead pressed into the wall.

And I know I will fall down before the walls that are holding my head ever do.

I WONDER IF 'CLIVE JACKSON' IS THE NAME OF A REAL PERSON (IT HAS TO BE)

Hatred towards other humans is a form of infinite kindness.

I heart hatred towards other humans.

I heart anything that can't talk.

Realize you are more uncomfortable with yourself than anything else on earth.

Then understand why.

Then identify yourself in everything else.

Then never compare yourself again.

Usually, I don't realize the clothes I'm wearing are stained until I'm already out in public and it seems inexcusable.

I have let too many people embarrass me for it to ever happen again—I'm telling you.

There are burst capillaries where I pinch your legs.

I give you many gifts.

Not having anywhere to go.

I give that gift too.

You can come visit me but the way back is salt for shredded hands and knees.

I am having nowhere to go and it's a gift of mine, please come visit.

Your bone marrow makes my teeth bright. Your glass teeth break on my bones.

My birthday is May 26, 1983.

No repair.

I am curious as to how many paralyzed mice I could swallow whole before I'd feel sick and have to exhale their souls, in what I bet would look like green plumes.

No one but me sees the green plumes.

Tonight while I eat my dinner—sitting with cold feet on a couch that leaks white stuffing that attaches to my hair and stubble while I sleep—I will give each piece of furniture a name so the next time I talk to people I can tell them I was hanging out with objects that sounds like humans.

No repair. Countdown to being a green plume.Ending yourself while you're still young enough to be a gift.

LISTENING TO MY NEIGHBORS SCREAM WHILE I DO A PUZZLE

No one is here to help you, they're just afraid of what you'll do without any help.

This morning I ate a whole bottle of chewable multivitamins but I didn't become perfect like I thought I would, so I went back to bed.

I am wearing a bad-smelling shirt with a blue stain on it and I think it's from a pen—I need to become dead in your car real soon.

I love your ugly face.

I want to fuck you.

Drinking pine-scented floor cleaner will not get the demons out of you—it'll just make you have painful pine scented burps the next day.

Nothing is wrong, we just don't get along with each other.

Get your head off my lap, I have to piss. You wouldn't want me to piss on your head. Or if you would, then make that clear somehow, I don't want to make a mistake like that. I don't want to make a mistake like that.

I AM POSSESSED (NOT JOKING)

The stronger humans teach others to hate looking at their own bodies.

You'll never forget what I look like after I put my eyes close to your eyes.

When people say they wouldn't trade something for the world, they are being illogical because the world contains the thing they wouldn't give up.

Stay still while I bite a clump of hair out of your head—feeling horny about the clump's pressure stuck in my teeth.
Because I am very in love with the things I don't remember well-enough.

I AM NOT UPSET

Eating a peanut butter and jelly sandwich for dinner like three or more times a week results in disappointment.

No actually that's selfish of me to think.

Push me over, I'm done.

Our time together will end with one of us hating what has happened.

Our time together will end and I won't apologize.

Our time together will end.

I GET UNCOMFORTABLE AROUND PEOPLE WHO GET ANGRY AT VIDEOGAMES

There is a place in my mouth that I have bitten three or four times today and now it is just long strings of pulp and it keeps getting stuck in my teeth and I'm trying to increase my courage to just swallow the pulp.

You are the person who colors your eyelids so people call you pretty when you cry.

I am the person who cuts pockets into my cheeks so the tears' salt thickens my face.

Love will heal the world.

I STILL HAVE ALL MY TEETH, HOMEY

Instead of a regular funeral, just duct-tape my body to a mattress and throw it into a forest preserve. I don't want to be any trouble.

Make up a symbol for your genocide. Some people will think it's nice without understanding it.

All of your relatives and friends are dying no matter how much you love them.

The same is true no matter how much you hate them.

At the age of 25, the bones of the human body fully harden, losing their pockets of air.

At the age of 26, I have become a pocket of air.

And I'm worried that there is a place bigger than earth, and that it will find me and I'll accidentally breathe it in, and that it will stay breathed-in—or that it has already happened and that's why I thought of what I just said.

Minus everything for me.

The air sews down what you leave behind in case you turn around and want to stay the same.

Trouble.

EXPRESSIONLESS DIGSUST IS MY NATIONALITY

If I bite you and all my teeth break out, I will thank you because you'll have shown me my teeth are bad.

Don't say thank you, it looks pathetic.

If you strangle me, your fingers will break on my neck. And I will thank you for reminding me. And you'll say thank you back.

I pick a tree out of the ground and stir the sky with it then put the tree in my mouth and see what it tastes like—but I don't tell anyone.

I need to find someone to buy walkie talkies with, and then go out into public and walk side by side saying, "Fuck you, over" back and forth.

THE BURGLAR

When I wake up and look around my room and remember everything about it and then decide to go back to sleep, it's the greatest feeling there is.

When I wake up on the couch and look around and decide it's time to go to my room, it's the greatest feeling there is.

When I am walking down the sidewalk or just sitting in the library and I remember that I will experience the same kind of days for millions of years, it's the greatest feeling there is and my dick leaks dirt.

You will find me and shake my hand when you realize what it means to be a purse filled with glass pulverized into dust—randomly combed by a small wind of self-hatred—and you will love me.

When I wake up, you will find me and shake my hand—having realized what it means to be a purse filled with glass pulverized into dust, randomly combed by a small wind of self-hatred—and you will love me.

I AM HERE

I am here and I just jumped to try to get away but earth pulled me back really fast and that makes me feel needed yeah.

I am here to secretly poke a hole in your leather couch so it loses value but you know nothing about it.

I am here to be an example of a washed-out fuck.

I am here to get high on my own bad mood.

I am here and the bugs bite my body while I am sleeping.

I am here and it makes everything feel like a terrible obligation.

I am here and I am pretending to sleep.

I am here to spend my life sharpening a knife that I use to cut my head off but then end up dying of old age a few inches into my neck.

I am here, and every time I think about it, I get grossed out.

Inner beauty is yours when I spit in your mouth.

SLEEPOVERS AT SOMEONE ELSE'S HOUSE ALWAYS SCARED ME WHEN I WAS YOUNGER BECAUSE I THOUGHT THE OTHER FAMILY WOULD SURROUND ME AND KILL ME

I bought you a balloon shaped like a star and I'm waiting until it barely floats before I give it to you.

There is nowhere else except for right here.

And everyone is trading air.

Sexual intercourse is here to stay, or some-shit.

You're an idiot if you want to play a role in anyone else's life.

You're an idiot if you think I won't glue your mouth shut and then open it by pressing my fingers in slowly.

You're an idiot if you approach the animal with the big jaw holding a toothbrush.

And the things you know will eventually be upsetting, are always the things you could never imagine being that upsetting.

Sexual intercourse is here to stay.

Don't get to know anyone.

Don't be ok.

Don't close your eyes to the long ladder of humans who you will never say hi to, and who will never say hi to you.

Don't go to sleep.

NOBODY CAN CONTROL ME

I am working towards making the walk to my grave the most unbearable and most solitary it can be.

And I don't feel sorry for myself.

I saw the words, "Happy birthday, Michael, we love you!" chalked on someone's driveway and it upset me for some reason.

I'm better than you at sitting still and looking at things.

I'm better than you at leaving my bed unmade.

I'm the best person ever at feeding goldfish, and smiling at babies.

So suck my dick I guess.

You wanted something from this piece of writing, but no, suck my dick.

PIECE OF WRITING THAT IS TONALLY DIFFERENT AND ENDS THE BOOK

Yesterday I realized home is the greatest enemy I will know.

Nothing can resolve the feeling that I am always far away from everything else and with every move I increase the distance.

And with me—with everyone—I realize I have changed, or will change the way I am looked at and replace it with something else.

And once done I will always see that something else for the way it moves in and out of my gross hands and mouth.

I'm not even sorry for myself, I just am. Un-disgraced ceaseless anger, wanting something, not knowing it by name and having wanted it for a while and that while having been sometimes sliced by pause, sometimes else made horribly present but either way, I know, I put too much hope in not having to tell anybody anything, or maybe constantly having nothing to tell.

There is a point at which the frequency and nature of your communications come close to actually forming a relationship and it is that point I have searched out with scientific care.

I give myself a headache by looking at myself in the mirror real close, but I do it well.

And the bad people will steal from you, even if you become

the bad people.

The bad people will steal from you even if you taught them how to be bad people.

There is only one way to imagine things.

And I am part of the thing imagined.

The lesson I learned from the times I thought you were going to say something but didn't, is a lesson I don't remember. Which is part of the thing imagined.

I try hard not to make a difference.

I can only imagine things one way, not having to tell anybody anything, or maybe constantly having nothing to tell.

Yuh huh.

NO ONE CAN DO ANYTHING WORSE TO YOU THAN YOU CAN

THE MIDWEST

Walking to get my paycheck today, I expected a hand was going to come out of the gutter and grab my ankle and then two eyes would appear inside the grate, with a voice saying, "Hey, just kidding, how are you."

Many of my recent thoughts involve someone who lives in a sewer becoming an important part of my life.

Many of my recent thoughts involve someone who will never become an important part of my life.

There have been times where I've reached into a bag of trail mix and found only the broken pieces at the bottom then put my hand over my face and said, "Oh god" real slow.

There have been times I've barely avoided a lasting relationship.

Or survived a beheading because I've shrugged.

I've seen a crowd of people in my head and the whole crowd points at me, saying, "Ewww" and is then quiet.

And the quiet is always worse than the "ew."

Niceness towards others is a measure of your own insecurity.

Isn't it terrible.

To be caught being someone in front of another someone.

Do you remember how terrible that is.

I don't think you do.

(Just kidding. I mean, sometimes that's probably accurate, but I don't know.)

Congratulations on being more hurt than anyone ever.

Congratulations on evolving any hurt-flinching into a look of celebration.

You should study the evolution, and become famous by explaining it to large crowds of people.

Would that work.

Would that even fucking work.

Right now, there's at least one other person thinking about cutting someone they know in half, like a magician using a saw—only without any illusion—without any saw—and this person is someone the magician knows—and this person has taught the magician the trick.

Sometimes things are done when you say they're done—and sometimes before you even notice.

Taking the garbage out at work yesterday, I saw a piece of the Chicago skyline visible through the high fence surrounding the dumpster area.

It made a puzzle piece of buildings and empty space.

I imagined being able to plug in the piece anywhere else without anyone noticing the difference.

Yes and I imagined I wouldn't argue about being the same piece.

When I got home from work, I lay down on the stained carpet, on my back.

And watched the shadow of the ceilingfan spinning.

And it looked like some kind of winged bug that's not going anywhere.

Not going to go anywhere.

Basically, I'd love to catch someone trying to scissor my noose uninvited.

I'd love to write the invitation.

Basically, it'd be cool if dying were just shrinking into absolute gone, at a pace relative to not wanting that to happen.

And yes—if I knew I'd never get arrested for it—I'd set a random apartment building on fire as soon as I had the chance/equipment.

That's just a little bit about myself.

All I know is, you have to imagine a piece of dynamite exploding inside your skull cavity—so you don't actually have to do it yourself.

Game over.

Feeling fake is the worst.

And the final score is the same as it started: zero to zero.

You will necessarily be liked and disliked by a certain amount of people.

And there is no need to do anything to change that amount.

Statistics.

Game over.

Hi.

Hum the same anthem to yourself when you're alone, as the one you hum to yourself when taking off the clothes of someone you don't like anymore.

And start over whenever you realize what you're doing.

The problem is not having to find a way back to the start, but thinking you have to find a way back to the start, or thinking that the start is still there.

It's like, the first person to draw a picture of a fire ended up with a picture that looked exactly like a picture of the first person trying to draw a fire and if I stop now I'll be admitting both that I'm done and that I never started.

How many times have you wanted to drown the person closest to you.

Be honest, you think about people drowning.

It's ok.

In second grade I cried because I was doing a long-division problem and there was an abnormally large remainder and my teacher leaned over my back to help me but I hid my face from her and a really big teardrop fell onto the problem and she wiped it off the page with her hand like it didn't bother her. For real though—now, I'm fucking awesome at division.

Anyway, drown yourself.

There's still plenty of time to do what doesn't need to be done.

And even more time to decide on ways for it to be done next time.

Enjoy the feeling of "next time."

"Next time" is a good feeling.

"Secret hate" is a good feeling too.

And it's not the burning that hurts when you light your head on fire, it's the smell of the shit you almost said accurately that hurts.

Fucking dare you not to care about anything.

Fucking dare you.

Global warming is good because I like playing outside.

Yes, and I hope you put your shithead-pose away for a little bit; it's getting old.

You're hated.

Apologize as offense.

And my ghost will return to begin the million-year war that is fought using only waterguns and pinches.

And if you think about it, everyone is cursed.

Everyone is cursed when they think about it.

A smiling mouth is a coffin.

And there is enough dirt to cover everyone who is living or will ever live.

And that will always be true.

You give yourself a smiling eulogy and the real you is the one who hears it dully from underground inside a wet cardboard box lined with garbagebags.

And that will always be true.

Don't think about it.

When I throw myself into the garbage I wear gloves, so I don't accidentally touch the garbage.

At the gas station last night, the guy working the register had so much greasy white armhair, that underneath the fluorescent light it looked like a time lapse video of some type of wet fungal growth on a rainforest floor somewhere. And I wanted to be transported to that rainforest—where I'd stand in place until I fully blended in.

Hopefully, youth is almost over.

Because the world looks different every time I look at it.

And so far, there's only a constant mood of suspension—a suspension of always being slightly-late to live the life that's been happening.

Hopefully, it's almost over.

Because when I distill my youth all that's left are the small enemies I've quietly imagined.

Imagined them injured in ways no one would believe.

Bernhard Goetz, get me home.

Bernhard Goetz.

My response to any crime against me is reversing the crime.

Reversing it, and increasing its painful end.

And I feel awesome.

Feel better than you do, promise.

I'm already there.

Bernhard Goetz, get me home.

I'm already there.

Today there was part of a graham cracker on the sidewalk and there were ants all over it!

And it made me realize I'd reached the last level.

And in the last level, you are given an already slightly-finished puzzle comprising infinite square-shaped pieces that you try to move around a little to complete, but only end up turning into a new picture that seems like it could never have happened from where you began.

In the last level, no one is watching you and you can do whatever you want.

But you're a terrible person, and you know it.

And at a certain level you just keep hoping you never reach the end because you don't want it to end—you keep thinking, "This can't end."

My head is empty when asked what I want.

Always feeling "maybe."

Always focused on something that soon enough won't seem important.

Always leaving the breast red from my stubble.

I do an impression of other people but I only copy the alive part.

Which is a talent.

Always maybe.

Facedown dead, I do a new salute.

And the salute looks like surrender to some.

Some people work harder on inventing ways to appear too pathetic to want to injure than they do on ways to injure.

Some pray to be invisible.

Have become invisible.

Through slowmotion wincing.

And new kinds of self-arson.

I've seen them make it look easy.

It's a bigger opportunity to fall into a hole than it is to be asked to make one.

You know that, I know that.

This sucks.

Fucking dare you to show up at my funeral.

Fucking dare you.

Fuckety fuck fuck it seems way too easy to poison an orange (syringe full of poison, duh).

I just made a list of people who are assholes and then I deleted it.

Sew together your discarded garbage-parts and make them into a robe you keep open down the middle so we can fuck whenever we need to.

Whenever we need to discard some garbage.

Fake personalities.

And no confidence.

I'd love to cut your face open with the smaller blade on a swiss army knife.

But who wouldn't!

A good method for maintaining even a little self-respect is yelling "No" in someone's face once or twice a week when asked something.

Like if someone asks you to pass them a napkin—even if the napkin is right by you—just yell, "No" in that person's face, while continuing to make eye-contact.

You have to hate others just-enough to be a better person.

You have to hate yourself just-enough for the same reason.

Getting a shirt out of my closet this morning I felt too miserable to unbutton the shirt so I just pulled down on the shirt and the plastic hanger broke.

Now I only have two hangers left.

I stood there and said, "Only two remain."

And even though I haven't thought about it too much, I'm pretty sure hangers are dumb, don't you think.

Necessary-relationships are the new fashion, don't you think.

Necessary-relationships are the new fashion—which means I'm fucking done.

I want to confuse a delivery person by ordering groceries on a weekly basis. Then whenever the delivery person arrives, I'll reach my fingers underneath the door and—using a raspy voice—I'll say, "Slip it beneath the door, my child."

This is good.

This is so good I am so happy right now.

This is my maniac youth.

And the maniac youth will never be over.

Because it is always just beginning.

27 years old and responsible enough to think being born is always an accident.

Fuck this.

Give me thirty-minutes and I'll feel completely different.

How many people have already left behind a tracing of what they were, in pursuit of some tracing of someone they half-assedly invented.

How many people found an old half-assed tracing and stepped into it, saying, "Perfect."

I want to be the kind of person who would only kill himself if given the chance to watch it.

Hung from the ceiling with a hook through my bottom jaw.

Wow.

I just remembered being eight years old and coming to a new school and mentioning to some kids that I liked to draw. They actually gasped when I said that and then they introduced me to the kid widely regarded as the best-drawer in the class and we both sat down and someone issued the challenge of drawing a turtle and we each made a drawing and I was considered the winner. It felt stupid. It felt awesome.

The most successful method for dividing people is to run through their held-hands, dividing them two by two.

Two by two, everyone becomes distance.

So get happy, motherfucker.

And get up early today, it's beautiful outside and there is even more beauty in the people you will meet and impress—so get happy motherfucker and put your hands on your own throat and think, "Almost there."

"You never smile."

"I've never seen you smile."

"How come you don't smile."

"Why don't you ever smile."

"Why are you smiling like that."

Everything is going real good though, yeah thanks.

Something's wrong when everyone likes you.

Seriously.

You're a failure if you choose an enemy outside of yourself.

You're a traitor.

And all traitors get buried young, even if they do it themselves.

You traitor.

Saying yes to something you know you can't do.

Stating facts about yourself that aren't true, you completely identify yourself.

My first reaction to not hearing from someone in a while is that s/he has discovered a good reason not to like me—a reason I'd immediately agree with if told.

And check this shit out—my main reason for not communicating is not wanting to bother someone.

Cool, dude!

Slamdunk, dude!

Because when dead, we all go to the same garbage pile—which is large and will only get larger—which is where we each get a single gold-star sticker on our heads and our heads in the pile make this constellation no one has a name for yet because first it has to stop growing—which is not going to stop growing.

Getting older means becoming more and more able to understand how other people feel and then feeling scared by it more and more.

Getting older means becoming less and less able to understand how other people feel and then feeling scared by it more and more.

I can't imagine my own face getting older.

Can't stop thinking, "This isn't for me, there is nothing here for me."

Apple juice is good but if you take a single sip of it right after waking up, it makes your breath smell extremely bad.

Whenever there's a silence between you and someone else—and you interpret the silence as unintentional—just say, "oops" then shrug, while still somehow seeming angry. And really mean it. It will help. I promise you, it will help.

I avoid things that will make me happy, because those things are the hardest to think about later.

Later is the worst.

It's time to hurt a thing that can't defend itself.

It's time to see the immense clear tendon that runs through all occurring things.

It's time to feel the worst.

If your toes are cold, put them in my hands.

If you're not sure if your toes are cold, then I don't know.

I have mistreated many people.

Watch me mumble explaining why.

Watch me not know.

When I was five, me and another kid who was five would show each other our dicks on the school bus home every day. Not sure why it happened more than once. Who knows!

But seriously I'm glad to have two hands still, because I can't choke myself effectively with one.

Glad to have two hands still, so I can beat myself up.

Kisses, baby.

Where is my underwear. I want to go.

Things that only make sense to me make the most sense.

Let me attack your family with physical violence.

Let me end all their lives.

Chicago Bulls. Chicago Blackhawks.

I dare you to share your life with anyone.

Even if by accident.

Fucking dare you.

No, don't share with anyone.

Become a tiny, plastic, nondenominational flag floating in an inch of old bathwater.

And don't share with anyone.

Even if by accident.

Because it's a bad feeling to realize you're being guarded by someone you'd never fully confess to, but that's half of any relationship.

But that's half of anything. Even if by accident.

Which means I'm through with you as a relation.

On to the goal of blending as evenly as I can with the world as material—mind no more.

And all the shapes I've seen are building the big last-shape that looks like everything altogether at once, and everyone's welcome in.

My mind is a glass square suspended in space somewhere between the sun and earth and when the sun goes through the glass, it projects all known life onto earth.

My jizz smells amazing, don't you want it on your neck.

For my contribution to the earth's death-collage, I'll be a small square of cardboard that has one mosquito leg still sticking to it from being killed by someone with a napkin.

For my contribution, I choose this face I make, which should be understood as a form of thanks that is not loud enough to hear.

For my contribution, I'm willing to mime either of the above, whenever looked at.

I encourage everyone to approach success then purposely stop right before it.

Then repeat that same action over and over, disguising it as success.

With thousands of ways to deflect others.

With no way to avoid it.

Dodge, deflect, or somehow defend.

Hurt others.

I encourage you to hurt others, and think of it as your greatest success.

"You're unnecessary," you say to yourself, turning on the faucet to brush your teeth.

"You are," you say to yourself, staring at the water in the sink.

"You're unnecessary," you say to yourself, anxious about nothing, scratching your head fiercely with both hands in the bathroom.

"You're done," you say, putting all your fingernails on the back of your head, then slowly pulling them forward into your eyebrows, standing in the bathroom, anxious about something.

"You're done," you say, looking at the floor.

"You are the floor," you say, still looking at the floor.

You begin a scream but stop it almost immediately.

My t-shirt has been on backwards for two days—only one of the days was when I hadn't yet noticed.

Possession by depressed ghost.

I'm always poisoned.

And the poisons always work because they always taste good.

Self-obsession: Important if you're at-all full of shit still.

I've won in any way you can name, and also in ways you can't.

Gladly taste-testing new poisons without making a face.

And by the time somebody reads this, I will have covered a hook with sugar and pulled a bigger uglier person out of my insides.

By the time somebody reads this, they will have proven it.

So let's finally be friends—and taste a new friend's hook.

If we start now, we can do the wrong things over and discover the new wrongs that require a start-over and if we start now we will still be too tired at some point to do what we need to do to make sure we need not another start-over but to keep going.

And the final score is zero to zero.

Everyone tried real hard, so there's nothing to be upset about.

Which means I'm going to chug a glass of my own blood and sleep for an entire day then wake up feeling like nothing will ever be special again.

Fuck this.

The sound I keep hearing is like a word that is a lot of letters that don't go together, screamed into a canyon.

Anyway, hope you're doing ok.

Yeah yeah, I mean it.

I'm all right, I'm all right.

It's almost the end of summer.

Chicago, Illinois.

2010.

4:46 a.m.

Sweating.

Cramping, sitting crosslegged in my room.

Thinking about my future—which always ends up turning into a vision of my burnt corpse in an overgrown, dandelioned backyard in the Midwest during Spring, getting eaten by a malnourished german shepherd.

The Midwest is beautiful.

YOU HEAR AMBULANCE SOUNDS AND THINK THEY ARE FOR YOU

FIRST

You are a very real person when that is what you wish you weren't most.

You avoid phone calls.

You fail in yearlong increments that shake hands with their successors when their shift is done and then go home proud.

You think that all lives are an individual's strange insistence on choosing a lifetime of last words.

You have imagined yourself standing still, smiling as everyone around you drops dead.

You have a vision of a faceless woman sitting in a chair knitting the future and it is a long photo negative of everything that happens ever.

You have bad paranoia.

You wash your face after crying so you can just say, "No, I'm just tired."

You feel fine always.

You keep putting your hands in your pockets and then inventorying the things inside because you are neurotic.

You have nice teeth.

You see old birthday cards you've kept for some reason and each one joins the swarming sharp things that make pulp of your heart.

You see your own face in the swarm of sharp things that only looks for more hearts.

You stare at the ground while scratching your face and you don't know what you are doing.

You know you should be doing something.

You just want someone you trust to cut you open to prove there is no gravel inside.

You just want to make sure.

You have seen me begging and you like it.

You admire yourself and you like it.

You hate when life reminds you it is really happening.

You are older now than you've ever been and it is not something you look forward to continuing over and over endlessly.

You are very real when that is what you wish you weren't most.

You hear ambulances sounds and think they are for you and you like it.

SECOND

You have never approved of yourself so you bother other people to do it.

You are an invisible trail of replicating statues each more fun to be around than the last.

You never help out people as much as they help you and that's the underside of something even uglier and it bothers you.

You have dumb hands.

You go to public areas and you expect people to group up and tell you you add nothing and you should leave, and you are willing to congratulate them on being right.

You don't argue.

You just ate so much cereal your stomach hurts bad.

You mention when someone else has stolen a relatively worthless pen because you have principles.

You think principles are real.

You eat things even if they aren't fully microwaved because you don't deserve any luxury.

You are the most beautiful motherfucker on the planet forever times the square root of 78,889.

You seem like a servant to someone you hope eventually asks you for something, for anything.

You get dead so slow.

You lost all your hair but I still love you.

You will feel pain.

You will not learn from it.

You will be mistreated by people, because somebody has to do it and at least you get to pick who.

You congratulate yourself on being right.

You are married to trying to defend yourself and you have soft gumlines for weapons you motherfucker.

You get preferential treatment in your own bad afterlife.

You are right to ruin yourself now so the afterlife will be a handicapped parking space.

You will not learn from it.

THIRD

You are royalty when no one asks you to explain something you just said.

You aren't sure whether you have feelings or not but that's all part of the shrug you have performed in slow motion for your entire life so far.

You will continue this shrug.

You will be rewarded.

You should hold a contest where the donations are used to pay to have a plane fly directly into my head.

You should do things on purpose.

You keep people away from you on the train because you smell bad and look weird.

You do this on purpose.

You do half of your living actions on purpose and half on accident and the accident half begins to overproduce and you like it you fucker!

You think it seems like everyone else is living some kind of life that involves ideas that exist outside your world and when you look around you think, "'No hope' is a feeling I have a lot."

You think about the why of the why and a block of ice

surrounds your head.

You are getting taller and taller and sadder and sadder.

You jump off high things but always make sure to land in ways that won't hurt.

You have known the experience of dividing yourself equally among other people who only want to divide you more.

You seem all right but you will know the general habit of being avoided.

You will know my ability to avoid.

You will secretly compliment my ability to avoid.

You are proud that you can concisely and effectively tell people how to beat certain video games.

You have never said anything that I didn't hang up on my wall, I promise.

You haven't even felt a kiss yet, you motherfucker!

You are terrrible with three r's, you.

You aren't sure whether you have feelings or not but that's all part of the shrug you have performed in slow motion for your entire life so far.

You continue the shrug, waiting to hear an ambulance.

FOURTH

You have a recent fixation of imagining yourself doing a front-flip through a table and then just lying there laughing.

You laugh a lot and it hurts and you like it.

You have no sexuality at all.

You feel palpably more free when your phone isn't charged or isn't working.

You just ate a fudgesicle and it fucking dominated your taste buds and you keep repeating "fucking domination" in your head until it's senseless and it's time to go to bed already?

You are everyday and you like it.

You make friends with strangers standing on pieces of ice that are melting and you like it.

You are only bored because you hate yourself.

You only know what to do when no one is watching.

You always act like people are watching.

You are a big monster made of wet newspaper and you get pushed down every three seconds and no one's afraid of you.

You have no reason to remain alive.

You built a small dwelling in your closet with some hangers and a sheet and you did this to avoid people, not to have fun.

You never have any fun, you fucker.

You only talk to yourself.

You will not survive that one beautiful thing you discovered when you weren't even trying to look.

You would like someone to throw a shoe at you now—you would just go, "Thank you."

You miss a lot of people but it comes out as a strong miss of only one thing.

You own your own ideal and you hate it.

You should commit suicide twice.

You're older now than you've ever been and it's not something you look forward to continuing over and over endlessly.

You hear ambulance sounds and think they are for you and you like it.

FIFTH

You were only happy when you were like five or six and that's it, right.

You think there are enormous amounts of people who love you but just to be sure you don't talk to any of them.

You have weapon vocabulary.

You have weapon vocabulary but fingers too weak to work each weapon.

You are anorexic.

You starve yourself for days and then hallucinate.

You look at me if you think I won't be looking.

You look at the light patterns on your wall and you stay in bed because you are avoiding everything.

You are objectively pathetic and your sheets are dirty and how can you live like this.

You can live like this.

You live like this.

You can live like this.

You like it.

You like yourself for reasons others do not.

You don't connect with anyone.

You listen to me and that's why I keep you around.

You hate everything and you like it.

You want to die.

You never know what day it is.

You can't imagine taking your mind off anything.

You pray but you don't know it.

You get nervous the few times you're at the doctor's office because you are convinced s/he might (justifiably) hold you down and execute you for carrying some incurable disease that can't be explained but will be fatal to everyone else.

You like everyone else.

You like being alone.

You always give up when things get hard.

You have never loved anyone like it is possible for you to and you like it; you don't like it.

You will feel pain.

You will be let down.

You have no control over how clean your face feels.

You have no time to turn around and see what you've done.

You have no need to see what you've done.

You talk and all you hear is ambulance sounds and you like it.

SIXTH

You made up a game where the winner is always you.

You made friends with the walk home when you really don't want to be anywhere.

You wake up and do things over again.

You are over again.

You always impress me.

You will powerfully vomit when you realize I'm gone for good.

You will powerfully vomit when you realize it's the part that remains that hurts most, not what is gone.

You're older now than you've ever been and it's not something you look forward to continuing over and over endlessly.

You're a compassionate human and you make ambulance sounds for anyone who wants them.

SEVENTH

You think your life will be better once you learn to somersault out of bed.

You think a lot but never decide anything.

You decide to walk straight towards death with no emotion on your face and no hope to change anything.

You wear your own medical bracelets for jewelry.

You only make people upset now, what happened.

You think about what happened and think, "Of course that happened."

You are my friend and that means you will see me act strangely.

You are a stranger and that means you are my friend.

You couldn't kill me if I had a connect-the-dots over my throat (and you know I mean that as a compliment).

EIGHTH

You haven't been able to face the outside so many times you wonder what has happened in your absence.

You couldn't draw yourself if you became invisible and wanted to reappear.

You see people outside your window and you lean out the windowframe and go, "Hey, catch me ok" then jump before there is an answer.

You base your actions on whether or not they limit what you think freedom is.

You base your actions on whether or not they will result in situations you feel are embarrassing.

You can't say what you mean ever.

You prepare your home like there is going to be a big party but then you never invite anyone over and you like it.

You really don't care what other people think and it's not at all like it was when you said that but didn't mean it.

You want to mean it.

You want to know what you're talking about.

You want to know how to understand years.

You want to know something.

You want to know something?—you are a mathematical equation that begins with a bunch of meaningless signs and ends the same way but it looks like a lot has happened (and you know I mean that as a compliment).

NINTH

You think it would be cool if your hands just, like, fell apart as uncooked rice and then you didn't have hands anymore.

You think it would be cool if you never felt obliged to anyone else.

You don't know anyone else.

You think of how you would like yourself more if you had come into existence by washing up on shore somewhere.

You are not the point.

You hear ambulance sounds and think they are for you.

You think you're being punished.

You know that punishment is wrong because the punisher can always just teach (it's like, why be a dick, right?)

You know you need to be punished.

You have typical human reactions and you are relieved because you can't imagine inventing reactions for some things (you know that's a form of punishment and you accept it).

You have pressure inside your body.

You walk around your apartment and feel like you can't be comfortable if you stop moving.

You meditate on the thought of your head being a blood aquarium.

You hate other yous.

You look like everybody else.

You look gross and you like it.

You get horny in a way that feels more like sudden homicide.

You have plastic cocktail swords for teeth.

You lose your teeth so often in dreams you no longer have free time now.

You never have real relaxations.

You balance on one leg while thinking of situations to get into that cannot be escaped.

You extinguish yourself from all sides inward and it happens too slow to show.

You extinguish yourself from all sides inward and it happens too slow to notice.

You notice.

You have your own flag and it looks a lot like your slob ass.

You can't believe how well I am able to sincerely love something for a really short period of time.

You can't believe how much I owe a movie rental place for a

movie I didn't even rent.

You don't listen to me and I love it.

You see and hear terrible things and when you run diagnostics on yourself to see if it has mattered, you don't know what to look for.

You made up a reason to keep breathing and it's working.

You just put your pen into your mouth to get something out of your pocket and then when you reached to get the pen you knocked the pen up into your gums and it hurt a lot and now you taste blood.

You have a sweet pussy.

You have real feelings and I steal them.

You make me happy.

You plagiarize faces of uncontrollable worry.

You do things that later seem strangely significant.

You have no idea how much "no" there is in all things.

You have no idea how old you are now.

You're older now than you've ever been and it's not something you look forward to continuing over and over endlessly.

You hear ambulance sounds and think they are for you and you like it.

TENTH

You are upset because you can only ever control things too weak to really want.

You think "oops" is an apology.

You don't wash yourself often.

You wear the coal mascara of no-sleep.

You should spend more time with me, you should.

You like it when I say "wink wink" after saying something serious.

You like that every creator also creates by letting its creations die.

You are embarrassed by how hard you orgasm thinking about my broken legs.

You will be asleep soon and that's ok.

You are an ugly person and I care about you.

You know that caring is hurting.

You feel terrible when it's late and you realize "nothing to do" is a permanent state.

You deliberately think about terrible things that make you want to die.

You train to die without making a face.

You die without making a face.

You will be found dead.

You will be found hanged from a tree branch, twenty skinned-arms for a noose.

You will never find a branch strong enough to hang yourself.

You end up dying of old age because nothing else can kill you.

You end up dead.

You end up alone in your room talking to everyone you've ever known all at once and it sounds like ambulance sounds and you like it.

ELEVENTH

You are an expert at experiencing pain and maintaining the same look, the one that fools people who want to be fooled.

You are an expert at acting ok so you don't embarrass other people and you don't get embarrassed ever now, isn't that weird.

You make excuses for everyone and you are liked.

You make up years of your own life and you like it.

You keep backing up and the world is many folds high now.

You use names to refer to people in order to make them seem more significant.

You use everybody and feel bad about it, but even that is selfish, hmmm.

You have a feeling that you are the result of dirt slowly aggregating out of air, hmmm.

You only have friends if you think hard enough.

You only know one way to have fun.

You should have more fun, yeah.

You should be more peaceful, yeah.

You should fall down and start to smell bad and not tell anyone where to look.

You should lose weight and put it on your head until you sink far enough to feel comfort—right, you got it.

You should figure out your own way to give up, one that makes it look like you're still trying.

You can have all my shit, I don't want it.

You shoot a gun at your face and see no bullets, just a slow-growing red beam that bends when it touches your face.

You perfected a form of silence that is your own ambulance sound and you fall asleep to it.

TWELFTH

You relax by not letting anyone know how you feel.

You resent people who know how you really feel.

You solve your own problems first.

You have hurt feelings and they are sticky shreds of what was a mouth that tried to hold in a bomb.

You allow yourself to really care about things knowing they will be gone, and you justify it somehow (even though you know you only justify things you are too weak to just do).

You are fucking lame.

You are the kind of person who recites amazing facts so you seem amazing.

You are not human and this is coming from someone with self-esteem nil.

You look the way you are trying to look.

You look like you are trying to find your way out.

You're older now than you've ever been and it's not something you look forward to continuing over and over endlessly.

You hear ambulance sounds and think they are for you and you like it.

HUMAN BEINGS ARE TOYS

No time inside the sun's lifespan would allow you to train for one concentrated look of indifference from my face.

No time inside the sun's lifespan would allow me to relax this face.

I'm willing to sit in a room for decades to plan revenge on someone who accidentally bumped into me on the train.

And I'm willing to sit in a room for decades to get revenge on myself. Izzactly.

Somebody hold me upside down so only my top half is submerged in Lake Michigan—my breath will freeze it, and I'll become the popsicle stick for a large popsicle that tastes terrible.

When the goal is to taste terrible, the future is much more interesting.

No time inside the sun's lifespan would allow you to train to carry the weight of the things I only half-explained but expected you to finish.

I'm willing to be at home in the time it would take to wait for you to finish.

And I'm willing to be at home in the time it would take to wait for revenge.

Willing to get revenge on myself by making revenge a pursuit.

Izzactly. Izzactly.

In an alley walking home, looking for a rat to follow home.

On the sidewalk, handing a homeless man some hard candy I had in my pocket.

On a roof looking at the skyline, not feeling anything beautiful or hopeful, instead seeing a big sandcastle I want to kick once and ruin—only once though so the form slightly remains.

In the kitchen with the freezer door open, measuring it with a tape-measure to see if I can move in.

Outside the door to my room, hoping I can walk in and get my keys with my eyes closed so I don't have to see my stuff or anything else about me.

Outside the apartment door, holding my keys and deciding not to lock the door because I want to come back to someone sitting on the couch ready to mate.

Outside the apartment door, holding my keys and deciding not to lock the door because I want to come back to an empty apartment with a series of boxes made into a maze that leads me back out of the apartment.

Izzactly.

Amen for being a jobless outline of a human with no obligations to any of the other 6 billion people in the world who are human outlines with no obligations!

Amen for the dark gray dust on my blinds, otherwise no one would know I was here!

Amen for candy on a fishing pole otherwise I'd never catch gross pets!

Amen for me, assholes!

Amen.

No time inside the sun's lifespan would allow me to explain how happy I get sometimes.

No time inside the sun's lifespan would allow you to train to believe me.

No time inside any of this would allow me to train to do certain things over.

In the passenger side seat of a moving car with the door open, getting ready to let my feet begin to grind against the road.

In the passenger side seat of a moving car with the door open and my feet grinding against the road, turning to the person who's driving to say, "You don't need me anymore."

Smeared inside miles and miles of street-pores getting thinned down by tires.

Standing by Lake Michigan wondering if someone will pay me to keep an eye on the lake or pay me to just touch it once in a while.

Sitting on the floor in my room, knowing at best I'm a sliver in the hands of a person who's thousands of feet tall washing his/her hands in soapy water that is the combined sweat of all the times spent running around the block hoping it would create a giant hole and bring everything with it.

No.

On the couch, looking at my pants and feeling so happy they're mine and no one else's—and I've never been better dude I've never been better.

No time inside the sun's lifespan would give you permission to act like you do.

I'm willing to let everything be revenge on me.

Izzactly. Izzactly.

How are you though.

At home, wondering where my next home will be and how much I will remember to miss this one once it's somewhere I can't be.

At home, ready to start throwing the furniture out the window.

At home inside the time it would take to manufacture a way to show the whole world my asshole at the same time (there has to be a way).

At home in knowing I'll never do it.

At home inside the time it would take to train to become your best friend.

At home in knowing I'll never do it.

In the parking lot, wondering if there are enough names in the world to give to all the little rocks, wondering if I have enough time to think of names.

Anywhere else, looking at people and waiting for them to initiate a conversation.

At home inside the time it takes to manufacture a way out of a conversation.

In the bathroom with my shirt off, admiring myself in the mirror.

At the Van Buren Bridge, watching traffic go beneath me and wondering if I can jump down and run along the tops of the cars.

At the Van Buren Bridge, laughing after I imagine how I'd land on the first car and fall violently to the ground, smashed and limp.

Smashed and limp, izzactly.

No time inside the sun's lifespan would allow you to train to become this smashed and limp.

No time inside the sun's entire genealogy is long enough to measure the length of the nap I want to take, only fifteen minutes after waking up.

And shit, I give you cpr every night then wait again for your lips to be blue enough to match mine—then repeat.

And shit, somebody has to love the dunce-art of my face when it shows I forgot what I was about to say but I don't care that I forgot and that's my revenge, izzactly.

I come from the grinded-jaw of planning revenge on everyone. And also from the first look of doubt on your face, coming out newborn.

No time inside the sun's lifespan would allow you to train the muscles that died with that look of doubt.

Feeling gross.

Can't wait to slowly finish this hospital I'm building around myself—it looks really nice, it does.

Standing in the kitchen, drinking water and leaning against the sink, looking out across the tops of apartment buildings at an advertisement for cell phones on the side of a building across the street.

Setting the glass in the sink and going to bed.

Inside a room that is inside an apartment that is inside how I think about where I am, that is inside everything I look at, that is some form of saying the same thing—always saying, "Don't touch me."

Inside someone else's body as their unborn, sideways and stuck, my legs numb, with a brittle skeletal frame made of stucco.

And I've never been better.

Never been more brittle.

Achieving a level of calmness that's a crime to others.

Amen.

So cheer up.

Cheer up and don't be disappointing today.

No time inside the sun's lifespan would allow you to train to accept that you can't help some people.

So cheer up.

And don't be disappointed.

On the Brown Line train, with no one else in the car except a man using a brown paperbag for a pillow.

On the Brown Line, with just-enough energy to get home and walk to bed and fall asleep before I even fully lie down.

In line at the 7-11, feeling the people behind me staring at my neck.

In the alley behind the 7-11, eating the food I bought and feeling like the best human alive, completely serious about it.

In the alley thinking, "Yes" at a low-volume 3,482 feet towards the center of my head, which then echoes out and goes quiet by the time it reaches my face.

In the alley behind the 7-11, deciding it's time to walk home and be there.

Halfway home, deciding to live beneath a car parked on the street.

Halfway under the car parked on the street, deciding I can't fit.

All-the-way to deciding to accept whatever happens, in whatever way it happens.

At home in deciding to accept whatever happens.

At home in my room sitting on the floor moving the upper

half of my body forward and backward, saying, "yes, yes" over and over.

Amen for endless life experienced every second!

Amen!

Amen for the disgust I've saved so long it can't be defended against, and amen for the people I use it to attack!

Amen for attack! Oh, I know!

Amen for the weakness of people who made attack something weak.

I come in my pants when I hear the first skull-shot of an attack.

I come from the same body whether it's the one that wants to shoot you in the skull, or the one who'd use gum to blow a bubble in the bullethole, taking you to your sky retirement.

And no time inside the sun's lifespan would allow me to word my apology right.

No time inside the sun's lifespan would allow me to get this right.

No time inside the sun's lifespan would allow me to try to make it better.

Every time I wake up there is a terrible feeling of being doomed never to love anyone.

And my lips are bloody from kissing my own ass so much.

Amen.

Izzactly.

I've been negative to myself more times than necessary and now I can deal with anything else.

Been the weakness of not wanting to attack other people.

Been alone in my room, arguing.

I've made things quiet in my room, where no one can argue.

Have made things quiet, looking out the blinds at the snow on the roof of the building next door.

Have thought about snow as a fellow person.

I come from where I will come back, because I'd rather run small circles in one place than run in a straight line seeing new things over and over.

And it's not going to stop.

It's not going to stop.

No time inside the sun's lifespan would allow me to build a replacement.

No time to try.

I want to bend my leg a way it shouldn't be bent, just to impress you.

And I don't want everyone to be ok, no. Who wants that.

Upside down on the couch, listening to the ringing in my ears.

Upside down on the couch feeling tired.

Upside down on the couch, looking out the window at the moon and its quilt-like fluorescent corona.

Facedown on the quilt that is the moon's corona, sleeping off whatever I've done to deserve sleep.

Inside the quilt of the moon's corona, where everyone goes when they die, to hold hands and keep the quilt together.

The quilt that is the moon's fluorescent corona is either what I wrap around my head in the morning to make me look pretty or what burns my hands when I try to strangle it.

And the ringing in my ears is the sound of hands trying hard to grip a neck but slipping—always slipping.

All day, the question is, "How is this ok."

"How is this the result."

Izzactly, izzactly.

At home in knowing American youth is over.

At home in knowing it's time for us to die off.

At home in knowing the fun will not happen again.

Don't be mad, just believe.

I'm willing to be a police officer around you—and to trade places whenever you want.

I'm willing to write down all the rules and sleep with my arm over them.

Willing to get revenge on people I watch from far away enough to go unseen.

To get revenge on people by staying away.

In conclusion, I'm willing to allow a picture of my corpse to be used for a commemorative plate that's sold at major retail stores.

At home, eating my own heart off a commemorative plate that has a picture of my corpse on it.

And after I get this belt off my neck, I put it around yours.

And after the belt is off your neck, it's back around mine.

And after I get the mail, I put it into the pile where all the other mail is and one day someone will find the pile and study it.

No time inside the sun's lifespan would allow the earth to create a bigger asshole than me when I'm trying to act real.

No time inside the sun's lifespan would create a big enough pause to explain why I never forget and why I never forgive.

I forgive by progressing to other things to concentrate on never forgiving.

And there will be many new decades of no forgiveness.

Izzactly.

I'ma never let it end.

I'ma keep you alive through a thousand painless deaths, to finally enjoy the last one.

Be my entire family.

Amen.

I'm willing to let my body be the wrappingpaper for a person who will be average always.

I'm willing to average out the times people have made me dumb and be the average and be made dumb again.

Living like this feels easy. Only, not at all.

No time inside the sun's lifespan would allow you to become brave enough to try to live like this.

In my room, sitting alone and looking out the window trying to remember what I was just thinking because it seems like it will change everything.

On a bench at the park, feeling two drops from a far-away sprinkler, thinking it has changed everything.

In the bathroom brushing my teeth, naked with a hand on my hip and getting ready to go to bed—getting ready to change everything.

Waking up and changing position in bed because everything is an idea I maintain by staying awake.

On the bus, sitting next to people and trying to change my hands into giant knives so I can cut my legs off and throw them at the bus driver.

Waiting for today to be done fucking someone else over so it will be my turn.

Please give me a turn.

No time inside the sun's lifespan would make me regret my turn.

And thanks.

Thanks for turning away from me when I pinch my eyes closed with my fingers and thumbs, trying to be molecule-small.

And thanks for opening your mouth on me when I expand apart—I'm hard to keep combined.

And thanks for showing me how to fall in and out of a personality and make it look like a trick.

Thanks for showing me how to be skinny and how to fall into the areas where other people's plans broke up.

And for not telling anyone else that it was me who broke up all the plans with a strong commitment to being a miserable fuck.

And for showing me what most other people are like.

Thanks for showing me the basic shape of my eventual corpse.

Thanks.

Because I never knew the sun's lifespan would let all this happen.

And I never pushed anyone to do anything—I pushed them to make them fall down and possibly get hurt.

And I never move because I'm too heavy to push.

No time inside the sun's lifespan will erase enough things to make space for me.

Fuck yourself.

What is the lowest amount of water needed to drown me.

What is the lowest amount needed, and do you carry it in your cheeks.

No time inside the sun's lifespan would give me enough baths.

I'm willing to say this to anyone I meet.

Willing to get revenge on myself by letting anyone listen.

I swear loudly inside my head, but on the outside I stay quiet.

On a concrete park bench, trying to figure out what day it is without having to ask someone who walks by.

Walking by someone on a concrete park bench and not making eye contact because it looks like s/he is about to ask something.

At home, sitting alone in the kitchen with a hand on the table and a hand on my thigh.

At home, sitting alone in the kitchen with a hand on the table and the other hand over my face as my face is piecing in a way I can't control and don't enjoy.

No time inside the sun's lifespan would allow me to train to control or enjoy it.

At home, pacing around the carpet and not finishing any thoughts.

Under the carpet is the script to my entire life and I wrote it by putting broken rocks on my feet and pacing the room.

I'm willing to read the script over and over as a form of revenge.

At home in this kind of revenge.

No time inside the sun's lifespan would allow me to train to be at home in this kind of revenge.

A SHIELD MADE OF NAPKINS

1.

AAAAAAaaaaaaaaaaaa….. (That's me falling into a pit of some kind.) …aaaaaaaaAAAAAAAAAA (That's me joining you in the pit you're in.)

2.

I still get scared of the dark but it doesn't happen as often now. When it does though, it seems a lot scarier. Like maybe if I just allowed myself to get scared more times, each time would be less scary. Huh, that's something to think about.

3.

A hurricane of knives that kills people and their relatives. No. No, a hurricane of knives that never comes into contact with anything but the ground. Be either one, but know which one you are. And yeah, all the knives still in your back, just leave them there; they make good steps. And yeah, your fingerprints are on some. Your footprints too.

4.

Some people don't polish, they scuff. Some people avoid me because I manipulate them, and it feels uncomfortable for us both when we let it happen. Feels uncomfortable when we notice we're letting it happen—but we let it happen. Making friends. It's satisfying to see some accidents happen, without ever doing anything to effect them. Equally satisfying to make them happen. To polish them when you're done making friends.

5.

The date of my birth is two my-selves grafted face to face, taking almost three decades to revolve and align into what I am now. And what I am now is facing forward and feeling faceless, wow. Keep facing forward. Keep going, keep going. North America, I hate you.

6.

Wow, the highest level of disgust is finding no difference in anything. Wow no, the best is making there be no difference. Anyway—who's in your army, and who will eventually come to mine. I want to know. No, I already know. Wink wink. Isn't it nice not to feel needed. It is.

7.

Guess what. When you work on making yourself better that just means now you're always disappointed with everyone else. You work on making yourself better, then try making everyone else better in ways that—ultimately—hurt all involved. And by then you have to start over because you've become the kind of person you want to make better. Goddamn, eww. So many shitty times. So many shitty times.

8.

Seriously though, it's very hard for me to actually enjoy anything. The real fun is in ending old fun. Or finding new fun. It's the same either way. I just want to fuck all the time.

9.

Who wins when you play hide-and-go-seek with everyone else and you don't tell anyone else you're playing? Who wins is everyone! And "Eyes-closed" is the best way to hide don't you think. Hard to admit some things, don't you think. Hide-and-go-seek is over when everyone thinks they're the ones supposed to be hiding.

10.

Sometimes it hurts when I orgasm, sometimes feels like nothing, and sometimes feels good. In conclusion, most people always keep a better version of him/herself in mind so the one they actually are is always not that good. In conclusion, you lose. Feeding yourself rust-colored shit with a small garden-shovel. Scraping off small bites with your front teeth.

11.

(Phrase-equivalent of the physical space separating one person and the person the first person won't apologize to.) (Phrase equivalent of feeding yourself rust-colored shit with a small garden shovel.) (Phrase equivalent of the smallest bite possible.) (Phrase-equivalent of a crayon drawing of a man falling backwards into his own grave giving the "thumbs-up" sign with both thumbs.)

12.

"Sleeping in tears" is a thought I have, right before thinking, "That's a dumb thought, you dummy" and the feelings equal out again. Half-undone and half-newborn.

13.

Just want to study a corpse and make cuts on it and use glue to seal the cuts so everything looks fine again. Yeah. So many shitty times. So many shitty times. This is not the first and not the last shitty time.

14.

Mate with many—and let someone else deal with the mistakes. And tell them they're honored to be allowed the duty. Mate with whatever. When was the last time you said you'd enjoy a day when it came and then just let it pass. And when last were you unable to sleep because there was something undone but you didn't know what.

15.

Sadness. There's lots to be sad about. Lots and lots. Each lot supported by a version of yourself incapable of changing the situation. (It's terrible, I know). But there's a way to accept everything you wish you could avoid, and the way is a sideways route as-yet not-attempted because it smells exactly like, "I already know." Don't let anyone interrupt your sadness.

16.

Two kinds of public death: Being completely ignored, or: Being made a cause to kill. And death is when your corpse dreams its life back in exact detail, all the way to the return point, so what.

17.

Own nothing others want. Have more than others own. And if helped, assume it's accidental.

18.

The dedication I have in avoiding my room sometimes can be compared to a scientist working on some kind of spacecraft that will be used to extract samples from a planet too far away to have a shape or name yet. The dedication others have in treating me like their room can be compared to the same kind of science. Son of a bitch.

19.

My wealth is imagined—best measured as what's been taken from another. It's tinsel I wear around my naked body, lying on some leaves, surrounded by people I treat kindly as father and hater, myself smelling perfumed by the smoke of their burning skin. And nothing and no one will interrupt the naps I take while still awake—daydreaming about a large field filling with corpses both burnt and perfumed. For the ones who hold in their histories out of spite—praise be to me, king shithead superior. Naked, with tinsel around my neck.

20.

So drunk right now on never having anyone to talk to. Drunk on backed-up ideas. Drunk on being a bully to myself with bad tension. Bad head times. Bad head times, man. Life-threatening paranoia. So what though. This bomb gets big by holding everything in, and don't you think this bomb will do a good job. This bomb will blow up stupid North America for good. For good, fuckers!

21.

(Phrase-equivalent of feeling so proud about a bomb you made, you jump into the air but then fall backwards and hit the back of your head on something and forget the phone number to the house you lived in when you were six.) (Phrase-equivalent of the face you make when you involuntarily think, "oh" in a negative way about someone.) (Phrase equivalent of the look on someone's face when they flex to refrain from saying, "oh.")

22.

Just tasted shit in my mouth for a second (not joking—it was weird).

23.

Some become new heroes because they do one thing and

never try again. Others are born with bad bacteria in their mouths, poison to slow old heroes. Because not everyone will like you—so don't oppose those who don't. Just be thankful that fact was made known. It's time to punch myself in the forehead until I'm bleeding. It's time. To wrap my dick with a dollar bill and fuck it into your dry asshole. Four of my fingers in your mouth.

24.

(Phrase-equivalent of a picture of a person lying in a carpeted hallway, head smashed apart.) (Phrase-equivalent of an American flag burned into someone's back, while that someone is naked on hands and knees.)

25.

Here's a prediction of the date of my death: August 14, 2027. (If that actually happens: amazing!!!)

26.

I've been able to witness myself as a disapproving stranger before—have told myself something I wish wasn't true and then again become a stranger. It's possible to be a stranger in someone's life but still introduce yourself to that person's life over and over. Getting along is unnatural though. For real, don't be polite.

27.

How to live a life that leads to: almost comatose. How to teach someone else to live that life. Today I was petting someone's dog, and for a second I thought that a girl I liked in high school had died and come to inhabit the dog's body. Laughing. Every laugh ends up feeling forced right at the end—because the end-sound is so fake because um because you realize you're laughing.

28.

Feeling taunted all the time. At all times feeling taunted. North America, I hate you. But I can be a good wife. Can eat the steroids out of any pose. Can imagine close friends dying. Can imagine having close friends. Can imagine a myself that hasn't come to this myself. Feeling taunted all the time!!!

29.

Is there progress in this shit life or is progress the part of the orbit that is not yet realized as a return. Oh yeah, I forgot—it will be clear once I stop acting like a defensive asshole. Because trying is tiring.

30.

Hello, my new arsenal is: I'm ready to fall down, I'm done. Hello, I sneak up behind you and introduce myself. Hello, my new wardrobe is the debris of you and yours is me lying on top of you. Sometimes ewwww and sometimes eww.

31.

You decorate the area directly in front of you by looking

at it—and you decorate with obstacles. Then, clearing all obstacles, you come to a clearing you'd like to decorate with all old obstacles. This is success and happiness. And you can have half, because the other half is always given back. Son of a bitch.

32.

New champion anxiety fulfillment big lifespan executive upsetting timespans gone solid. New champion isolation antifulfillment regiment unsuccessful friendship distinction made gold. Shit can get so bad sometimes, but the backs of dumb rivals are soft on my feet when I'm running my way across their dying bodies. New champion idiot interior gone clear and adopted.

33.

The newest kind of rolemodel looks calm while swallowing his/her sinking face. Standing still while swallowing the sinking face.

34.

Sometimes it really is the right thing to do to not get out of bed. Motherfucker, I already know, it's terrible. Too unhealthy to say no to new mornings. Not healthy enough yet. Need to get well. Need no more mornings. I'm murdered every morning. "Murdered every morning," is the shout of each new morning. Dumb generation after dumb generation. Wiping my feet on the backs of my peers. And keeping my back clean. I don't give a fuck anymore. New cleats will be fashioned from pieces of demolished skulls.

35.

(Phrase equivalent of the sound cleats make against a tile floor, when both are fashioned from demolished skulls.) (Phrase equivalent of dying twice at the same time because of how much you miss someone.) (Phrase equivalent of realizing you never miss anyone, you just feel bad sometimes being alone with a version of yourself that can't stand itself and thinks something will change that and that something is someone else.)

36.

I walked home in the rain today and there was still some snow on the ground and the rain was pushing the snow down and for some reason I couldn't stop thinking about my head just completely falling off my shoulders. And the sound it'd make when hitting the ground would be "piff" because it'd immediately become snow and get pushed back into the ground.

37.

Do you even want anything. Do you want to see me lying on the ground, breaths away from dead. Do you want to see your family die. Have you seen my version of earth, reduced to debris. And have you considered that on this debris we could sit—you as whatever you are, me as yours. Do you want to smash a grape into my ear and make my ear infected. Is that what you want.

Do you even want anything.

38.

(Phrase-equivalent of a picture of two people kissing with their mouths open, gagging.) (Phrase-equivalent of realizing you want to be somewhere else.)

39.

The kind of tired where it feels like your head is filled with hot liquid. The kind of tired where you feel happy. The kind of tired where you wake up laughing. Who wants my dick in their mouth, raise your hand. Hold it up high.

40.

It's like, at some time in the future I will look down and see that I'm wearing underwear made from a brown paperbag and it will be lovely—I won't question it, that'll just be it. It's like, it's easy to feel normal if you never think of one thing as something else. To be unafraid. And to stare mostly at the ground, even when walking around in public. And to not try any harder. Don't try any harder. Because you don't know what you want yet.

41.

Keep going, keep going. Keep yourself small enough to hide in most available faults. Keep yourself big enough to create faults when walking. Keep impressing no one.

42.

Real bosses shrink worlds by burning them. No, I mean, by forgetting them. Oops I suck. And um, it might be time to attempt a brutal homicide/suicide using a tool that will never work. Might be best to always use a tool that won't work. Might just be me but I regret my involvement in this timeline. Fucking shit. It's like, fucking shit—you know?

43.

(Phrase-equivalent of a picture someone took of someone else who didn't know the picture was being taken.) (Phrase-equivalent of the nickname for a person no one likes.) (Phrase equivalent of someone beaten to death in a parking lot.) (Phrase equivalent of the Chicago Blackhawks.)

44.

If you believe in an afterlife, kill yourself—it is good to be with what we love. Or even if you just like quiet, kill yourself—it is good to be with what we love. Find something you love and be selfish enough to want it all the time. Be selfish enough to be the kind of person who is wanted all the time.

45.

On my left foot there's a hard bump on a bone I broke a few years ago playing soccer and never got fixed. Sometimes when I touch the bump I remember that I'm never the same thing. And that I'll be the same thing when my life ends. And that life is going to end. And that life is a shield made of napkins.

A mask made of napkins. A knife made of napkins. A bow and arrow made of napkins. A forcefield made of napkins. A bra made of napkins. A butt made of napkins.

46.

Watching the way a person tries to say things by moving on to saying something else is more important than listening to each try. I can make sense out of a smashed insect. Smashed insects have histories. Watching myself make sense out of smashed insects. Watching myself make moves to get people less close and I've been enjoying the tries. Or no, I've been enjoying how I don't notice the tries until later. Haha—whoa—big difference!!! Distancing people like I'm smashing insects.

47.

Sad sad futures. Sad futures introduce themselves as new ways of living—and yeah, I'd like to live each one, each time. Live each one until its end.

48.

Do you want to learn the spirit of making someone else feel at blame. Do you want me to teach you. Is it time to take out our keys and hammer them together. It is!? Time to do something with an uncertain outcome and it's always time not to argue. It is.

49.

Hey, I like to focus on the image of myself burnt to death in my bedroom, with my hands up to my face, looking handsome like always. Kisses. No sex anymore, just kissing. No kisses anymore, just nothing. And the mood is either: immediately realizing everything is awful, or: immediately realizing I'm unsure. The move from one to the other is still something that's gone when I go to grab it. Gah-damn!!!

50.

A hammock of tits. A hammock of tits and me lying on it naked, with the oil of my unwashed body for cologne. I'm getting somewhere but I'm not writing down the directions. And I expect to be joined.

51.

I see other people and wonder if they've had the exact same thoughts as me and if so, would that be better or worse than otherwise. I see other people and have no thoughts. The worst feeling is hearing someone else express a thought you wish wasn't true but have already accepted. Money. Shit. BB gun. Death. Unmarked grave in the woods.

52.

I judge other people based on how quietly they remain camouflaged—or find ways to make camouflage out of what seems like a situation where there isn't any. Or find ways to steal my future. Good thing I have no future. Good thing you want my future to be yours!!! Good things have no future. Jeez oh man.

53.

I mean, I'm trying very hard to correct the things about me I think are wrong. Trying very hard. I don't want to avoid the quiet I know I have coming. Trying very hard. But have become weak. Weak—laughing in a way that feels good to me but bad to anyone hearing it. Because trying is tiring. But yeah, everything's ok leave me alone.

54.

We're ok if we're still attractive to people we find attractive. Oh yeah!!! (I just jumped up into the air and threw both arms upward, fast.)

55.

And there's real violence in the moment directly after permanently dismissing someone from any further decision you make. There's real hope in how motionless you can remain when someone does that to you. Keep going. Keep going until it becomes an honor to look up at the person who dismissed you. Keep going until you're in love with the taste of real violence.

56.

Hooray hooray. Hooray for life. Hooray for you and me. I'm open to every person who's open to me. I can be a good wife. Feeling taunted all the time, I can be a good wife. Standing at the center of an expanding circle, endless angles looking out at sad futures I haven't lived, but want to, spinning around with my eyes closed letting it happen.

57.

Crown yourself then kill yourself. And trust that there's no tool sharper than a crown broken into pieces then taped to a stick. No one can do anything to you that's worse than what you've already thought to yourself. No one can do anything worse to you than the things you've already done. No one can do anything worse to you than you can. Sho 'nuff.

58.

Seriously, you don't know how heavy you are until nothing holds you up anymore. Heavy is good. Going from an orbit that looks like progress to just lying on the floor motionless. Not asleep and not newborn. Just motionless, lips blistered from kissing your own ass so much. So yeah, watch me salute a fucking brick wall. How I salute a brick wall is my new religion. And newness is something that—thought out fully—recoils into an always conceivably-smaller thing. I'm going to retire already long past any wins. Long past, just to make sure. Have a nice morning, afternoon, and night.

GERALD MCCLELLAN
VERSUS
NIGEL BENN

HOW THEY GET YOU

Yesterday I was walking around Pilsen Neighborhood in Chicago, Illinois.

I passed by an abandoned lot and on the other side some bushes along the sidewalk started shaking.

A city worker wearing a neon-yellow vest came out of the bushes.

She held big garden shears, a handle in each hand.

She wiped her face with the shoulder of her neon-yellow vest.

Without looking at me, she said, "This be how they get you. Jumping out a bush atcha."

And I said, "Yeah"—like, "Sadly, yeah"—like I knew that was how they get you.

But, I didn't know that was how they get you.

The city worker whistled one note and kept clipping.

GUY WEARING THE PINK AND BLACK LUMBERJACK HAT

On the train this morning I sat across from a guy wearing a pink and black lumberjack hat.

His eyes were open very wide and he was talking to himself—laughing and stretching his neck out intensely, where you could see the cords/ tendons/whatever.

At a stop downtown, two middle-aged businessmen got on.

One sat next to the guy wearing the pink and black lumberjack hat and the other stood in the aisle.

The lumberjack guy talked to himself, stretching his neck out.

He stretched his neck all the way to one side and stared at the businessmen with his eyes fully open.

Then he said something and both businessmen laughed.

The businessmen continued to talk to each other.

One said, "Yeah so, what are you doing now then. Different project, or."

The other said, "No, technically I'm doing a multilevel, multi-tier project involving other smaller endeavors, so I have to see them through the transitioning period, yeah."

"Oh, that's interesting."

The guy wearing the pink and black lumberjack hat stood and walked to the other end of the train and sat by himself.

He sat there, laughing.

Talking to himself.

Stretching his neck out.

VITAMIN C

On the walk home from getting some vitamin c tonight, I had to wait for traffic before crossing Fullerton.

A little bit down the block, someone was looking at a pile on the sidewalk.

The person looked more closely at the pile then looked up at me and walked away, shaking his head.

I went over to the pile.

It was a blanket with something beneath it, blood on the sidewalk.

A note taped to the blanket said: "Dog was killed. Please do not move."

And I wanted to move it, but I didn't know where.

Maybe just pick it up and walk it down the sidewalk under the moon.

POPCORN

My girlfriend paid for me to go to a movie with her.

Standing in line to get drinks and popcorn, someone behind us said, "Excuse me."

I turned.

It was an old man wearing a baseball hat with the Chicago flag on it.

He was pointing at our stuff.

He said, "Uh, pardon me, what size was that you got there."

I said, "Medium, I think. Yeah."

He said, "Oh ok, medium, that's good" making the "ok" sign and nodding, "That's what I want, I'll get that size then."

"Yeah it's good," I said, distinctly unaware of what the fuck I was talking about.

I half-expected him to put his hand on my shoulder and say, "Son, what the fuck are you talking about."

While my girlfriend paid, the old man told me about the movie he was there to see and also what movies he wanted to see.

Then he referenced this older actress in an upcoming movie and how much he loved her and how—even at seventy years old—she could "still

walk it, still talk it."

He whistled once, rolling his eyes as if unable to tolerate how good she still looked.

"Yeah yeah," I said, smiling and nodding.

Been saying "yeah" twice as a response—not to mean "I don't believe you" but to say yeah twice.

"You bet," said the guy, smiling. "Alright then, have a nice night."

He took his hand out of his pocket and tapped my elbow, stepping forward to order.

"Have a nice night," I said.

Me and my girlfriend walked away.

We walked down a brightly lit hallway to get to our theatre.

I said, "Fuck, like, if I went out to a movie alone, I wouldn't want to bother anyone by talking to them. I'd stand there telling myself not to bother anyone. But then, he talked to me, and I liked it, so."

"Yeah," my girlfriend said. "Did you see how nasty his teeth were."

I didn't say anything.

Just walked down the hallway thinking, "Fuck you" then more like "fuuuuhhhh-cuueeee"—in a terrible, phlegmy scream—directed first at my girlfriend, then at her and everyone else, then back at me, with a "welcome home" of me not reacting at all.

PEAR

I got food at this place underneath the Red Line tracks in Uptown.

The place didn't even have a name—or the name was hidden by the train tracks or whatever.

Inside, I ordered and waited, leaning against the wall.

This other guy was on his cellphone, leaning his elbow on the counter facing the street.

He said, "Uh huh, I'eard ya. But you did it, right."

He listened.

The worker preparing my food looked up and said, "You can take whatever you want to drink from the cooler, man."

I went over to the cooler and took out a bottle of water, knocking another bottle over, which I picked up.

The guy on the phone said, "It hurt? It didn't hurt nah. Uh huh. Yeah, but he like it." He sniffed. "Ok den, come see me, come see me."

He ended the call and put the phone on the counter.

I stood there drinking my water, looking out the front window at Broadway Ave.

Lots of people walking by.

Someone opened the door and leaned halfway in then said something to the cellphone guy, handing him something.

The cellphone guy said, "That's why I got her though, she do that shit. Need people who do shit you need done, feel me?"

The worker was wrapping my food and putting things into a brown paper bag.

Guy leaning in the doorway said, "Ey."

The worker looked up.

"Ey," said the guy in the doorway, "Ha-bee-bee Boo-boo, what's good man. How'sya, um how'sya magic carpet and camel n'shit."

He and the cellphone guy laughed.

They slapped hands and hit shoulders together.

Cellphone guy said, "K, I be right outside den" as the other guy left.

The cellphone guy turned to the workers and said. "Aight, later boys, I catch'all tomorrow."

Then before he left, he held something up and said, "Oh yeah. Innyone wants this pear?"

He held up a pear.

"Who want it, now," he said.

No one said anything.

"Shit's good for you," he said. Then he said, "Fine fine" and left.

I wanted the pear.

But I didn't say anything.

I just couldn't.

THOUGHTS ON A BAG OF FASTFOOD I SAW IN THE MIDDLE OF THE HIGHWAY LAST NIGHT

Constantly overrun by cars, but never getting hit by the wheels.
Remaining intact.
Shaking from the wind of the cars speeding over, but still, intact.
Worst, remaining intact.

VIDEOGAME GUY UPSTAIRS

1.

The guy who used to live right above me played videogames a lot—sometimes for consecutive days, real loud during all times of the day.

He'd yell at the videogames and break things in his apartment while playing.

He'd yell, "Fucking goddamn stupid bullshit" and stomp on the floor a lot then there'd be a scary sound of something breaking/him screaming.

I liked him.

He was very creative with his swearing.

His swearing was always new and bold.

Like, it was always some variation of "fuck" with "shit" or "goddamn."

Like, "Fucking goddamn bullshit motherfucker I shot that motherfucker in the head."

Or, "Fucking bullshit, I blew that asshole up with a fucking motherfucking grenade."

His stomping was also impressive.

Seemed genuine.

Full of anger.

I felt the anger in each stomp.

If I had to guess, I'd say his stomps involved both feet at the same time, throwing his upper body backwards.

If I had to guess, I'd say his stomps involved imaginary heads beneath both feet.

And blood.

And death.

And motherfucking goddamn bullshit.

2.

The first time I went upstairs and knocked on his door to ask him to stop, he didn't respond for a few minutes, he just lowered the volume on the videogame.

When I knocked some more, he opened his door a little.

He looked very small and scared and tired.

I said, "Are you uh, playing videogames loudly and yelling a lot."

He said no, but that yes, he had heard it and then he said he thought that sound was coming from across the hall.

When I told him I lived beneath him and could hear like, stomping, and yelling too he said no, but that yes, he had heard it, and man, he thought the sound was coming from my apartment.

I didn't say anything for a little bit, just maintained eye contact.

Then I said, "Oh. Alright, thanks."

Walked back downstairs.

3.

A couple days later, he was yelling and breaking things really early.

I went back upstairs.

It was weird trying to think of what to say.

Are you supposed to say, "Hey, me again."

Or, "Remember me?"

I paused halfway up the stairs and thought of multiple scenarios.

Like—him answering the door and denying it again and me nodding, saying, "Ok, but this is your last chance" then I turn and jump down the stairs to the next floor.

Or—him answering the door and denying it and then I ask him to help me find the apartment where the screaming and stomping was coming from and then we become best friends as we solve the mystery of who's playing videogames and stomping and yelling.

Or—him answering the door, me nodding upwards and saying, "Need a friend?" then walking into his apartment and picking up a videogame controller and being his friend.

Or—him answering the door and me just running back downstairs, tripping down the last three stairs and breaking my ankle then hitting my face against the wall.

Or—him answering the door, me smiling and pointing, saying, "Hey, just wondering if you could stop screaming at the videogame you're playing" and then he says, "Of course, my child" and disappears into a pale blue light and I walk into his apartment and play the videogame alone and someone knocks on the door and asks me to stop yelling and stomping.

It'd be great if he was just doing a puzzle and he came to the door, opened it, then casually said, "Yes? What is it, I'm doing a puzzle" gesturing into his apartment where there was a partly-constructed puzzle on the floor.

But it didn't matter because he just turned down the volume when I knocked, didn't answer the door.

4.

The last time I interacted with videogame guy upstairs was right before he moved out.

He was playing videogames loudly.

Yelling and stomping his feet.

From my room right below, I yelled, "Shut the fuck up" so loud it hurt my eyes.

He turned down the videogame and stopped yelling and stomping.

Made me want to yell, "Pay my rent too, and buy me a fucking hermit crab."

ALMOST

When I went to cross the street today this guy grabbed my shoulder and held me back as a bus sped past, blowing my clothing up against me.

"Ooo-wee, watch it," he said, letting go of my shoulder.

"Man, it was almost my day" I said, with like, a distant/dreamy smile on my face.

The guy shook his head and said, "Good thing I got you."

I started to say, "No, like"—meaning to explain that he'd ruined something—but the "Walk" signal lit up and we both crossed, careful not to walk too close/at the same pace.

Very careful.

YO BUSINESS

On the way out of a donut place this morning, a woman sitting alone at a table grabbed my arm.

Her eyes pointed up at the ceiling in different directions, with bad cataracts.

She said, "Hey, now 'memba honey, I'n tell you this. Wh'ever you go," rubbing my hand and arm a little, "—always speak yo piece. Speak on yo business then. Ow k?"

I said, "Ok," nodding.

Her hand felt nice on my skin.

She smiled.

And then I was outside in the parking lot, deciding to button the last undone button at the top of my shirt, ready for anything.

PIGEONS

There are pigeon blockers along the beams and overhangs of most outside train stops in Chicago.

The pigeon blockers are strips of steel, with sharp upturned segments like saw-teeth.

Sometimes I'm just standing there waiting for them to come to life and fly at me, snapping open and closed.

Me running at first, then being like "No, why am I running" and allowing the jaws to close on me.

Except the teeth don't bite, they bend around me.

And it's just me standing on the subway platform with all this metal bent around me, and I say "fuck" before going back to wait for the train.

THOUGHTS ON WHAT I REALLY LOOK LIKE

Like, there's me, then there's a smaller me in orbit of the regular sized me. But the orbit is just a constant floating backwards, describing the regular me left in the distance. Getting more and more distant but still trying to describe. And the way it's described is how I actually look. And no one can see the process behind it.

FRIES

My girlfriend and I are walking her dog around Uptown.

It's really hot.

At a stoplight, I watch an old lady in the parking lot of a fastfood place throw an entire package of fries onto the asphalt for the pigeons and seagulls to eat.

And I start thinking about how I want to do that every day—to have that be the thing I did every morning—not read the paper, not drink tea, not make juice, not smoke a cigarette, not exercise, but go and buy a few dollars' worth of fries and throw them all into the parking lot for the seagulls and pigeons to eat.

And the pigeons would come down from powerlines and the seagulls would all come from the lake every morning, just to see me.

They'd all rely on me.

I'd be theirs.

How would I deliver the fries though.

Would I break the fries up.

Would I throw them down one at a time.

Maybe break them all up and throw them all up into the air like confetti for "one big rush."

What would I do.

We cross the intersection and keep walking.

I wipe my face with my shirt.

My girlfriend says, "My grandma died in a heatwave like this. She got really paranoid and wouldn't leave her apartment and then like, at a certain point, she wouldn't even let people in. Like she wouldn't let people deliver groceries because she was too paranoid to have the door open, even for a second."

Her dog walks in front of me to sniff something and I almost trip over the leash.

And I think about an old woman locked in her apartment, dying.

I imagine her lying down to die.

And then after she dies she wakes up as a seagull, in motion over Lake Michigan, following other seagulls to a fastfood parking lot where I'm throwing fries all over the fucking place.

QUIT JOB

I quit my warehouse job a week ago.

I was helping the head of security throw out garbage in the alley.

He'd just told me that last night when he was throwing out garbage, he saw a prostitute sucking someone's dick.

I said, "Oh yeah, so I think I'm going to quit."

He looked at me and said, "Oh shit, really. Ok." He was nodding. "Man that sucks though. We all really like you and everything."

"Oh man, thanks."

We threw out the rest of the garbage without speaking.

Then he noticed my boots.

My boots were brown but I'd colored them black with a permanent marker.

"I ordered black but then they sent me brown," I said, explaining it to him.

Then, before he reacted, I said, "Best of both worlds" and thought about how that didn't mean what I meant.

Felt like saying, "Hey just so you know, again, I quit."

And for about eight seconds, the idea of not having a job made me feel like I could do anything I wanted.

There was nothing I wanted.

RIDE WITCHO MAN

The last day at that job, I was in the breakroom eating a yogurt someone didn't want.

Talking to two girls.

One girl was sitting next to me, opening up a small lunch thing where you combine crackers with deli meat and cheese.

The second girl was standing by me, one hand on the back of my chair and the other hand completely bandaged.

She held her bandaged hand in my face and said, "This be from fightin' w'some A-rabs. Yeah. I's out wimma man and these A-rabs jumped him at a restaurant we was at. You know how them A-rabs luh to tussle."

"Ey do be tussling," said the girl at the table, turning her head sideways a little and looking at me as she combined a cracker with deli meat and cheese.

"Arabs love to tussle," I said, shaking my head no. "What do they do."

The girl with the bandaged hand said, "Yeah, they luh to tussle. So I buss my hand punching this A-rab dude" then in a higher voice, "cauz he was fucking wimma man, f'rill."

"You broke your hand on his head," I said, flicking a piece of pretzel off the table.

She smiled and hit my shoulder with her uninjured hand and said, "Mm hm."

The other girl got serious and looked at me and said, ""S'right, because you gotta ride witcho man."

"Hell yeah," I said, feeling in love with her.

Bandaged girl said, "Hell yeah."

Then someone else in the breakroom began a conversation

where people took turns saying what s/he'd do if s/he won the lottery.

When it was my turn, I leaned my chair back and said, "Shit, if I won the lottery I'd," —and I let my chair hit the ground, moving my head back and forth like I was trying to touch each ear to a shoulder, "I'd ride witcho man."

And the girl with the bandaged hand laughed and stomped the ground and her friend laughed and I laughed and when the bandaged girl pointed at me I just did this dumbass shrug, hands up, shaking my head no.

GIANT HORNET

I'm sitting on my girlfriend's couch staring at the wall, where sunlight projects the shadow of her dying avocado tree sapling from the windowsill behind me to the wall where I'm staring, right above the shadow of my head. And it looks exactly like a giant hornet hovering above me, the stinger waving. And I like it.

THE TRUTH ABOUT THE JACKHAMMER AT THE CONSTRUCTION SITE YOU'RE WALKING PAST

It doesn't matter if you try to encourage the jackhammer to fall on you from off a fifty-foot scaffold. Because the jackhammer isn't connected to your mind. You can try. You can think, "Just fall." But that won't help. The jackhammer will remain where it is. And you will pass by unharmed, every time. Less and less harmed.

MARCOS

I saw an old co-worker, Marcos, coming out of the liquor store at the end of my block.

He came out with two cases of beer.

He said hey and walked over.

He set the beer down and zipped his sweatshirt and picked the beer back up.

I asked him how he was and he said he was just coming back from his cousin's funeral and people were going to his grandma's place a few blocks away.

"Yeah man, my cousin got shot in the park," he said. "Sucks."

"What happened."

He said, "Dude comes up behind him and puts a gun to his head and, blam, shot him."

"Shit. For no reason."

"Ha, no. Cous' was banging. Me too, but I got out. That's why I can't go over like, on the blocks past Wilson and shit. They know me over there. They'on't like me over there ha."

Two guys walked past and one looked at the beer Marcos was holding and said, "Aw shit. Y'all finna DO it."

Marcos motioned with the cases and nodded upwards. "Yeah it's some sad shit, man," he said to me. Then he clicked his teeth and said, "But, shit."

"Well," I said. "Orale, pussy, let me get a beer."

He backed up a little, laughing.

We were both still alive.

"Fuck you, pussy," he said.

Whenever he smiled/laughed it looked like he had Down's syndrome.

SUBWAY

Today when I scanned my train card, I thought the screen said: "Fuck you," but really it said: "Accepted." Did I want it to say, "Fuck you"—maybe, maybe.

NICE JOB

I saw this guy park a giant truck into a loading dock off a busy Chicago street. He did it in one try, barely inconveniencing the other drivers. I wanted to yell, "Nice job." But I didn't want him to feel like I was trying to mock him. I thought about being more specific, like, "Hey man, nice job parking that truck in one try in the middle of all this traffic, that was good" but that seemed even worse.

A LIST OF HOW SOME BOXERS HAVE DIED

Rocky Marciano—plane crash, decapitated.

Corrie Sanders—shot in a bar robbery while covering his daughter.

Joe Frazier—liver cancer.

Sonny Liston—heroin overdose.

Paco Rodriguez—collapsed in a coma in the tenth round of a fight. His organs were successfully transplanted to five people.

Benny Paret—first person to die on national television when his opponent Emile Griffith hit him twenty-nine times in row before the referee stopped the fight.

Billy Collins Jr.—died in a [possibly] suicidal drunken car crash after one of his opponents, Luis Resto, fought with tampered gloves and tore Collins' iris, forcing early retirement.

Charlie Mohr—died during college tournament in the 1960s, ending all of college boxing.

Jimmy Garcia—brain damage.

Benjamin Flores—brain damage.

Becky Zerlentes—brain damage, first woman to die.

Randie Carver—brain damage.

Vernon Forrest—robbed at a gas station, shot seven times in the back.

Edwin Valero—hanged himself in his jail cell awaiting trial on charges of killing his son and wife.

Julian Letterlough—shot in the back.

Diego Corrales—motorcycle accident.

Arturo Gatti—unsolved, either suicide by hanging or murdered by wife.

Hector Camacho—shot, taken to hospital where he died for three minutes then came back to life, brain-dead, taken off life support at the request of his mother.

BUS THING

When I got on the bus this morning, it accelerated before I could grab something. I reached for a pole and grabbed it but it swung me around and I fell into the lap of a very old woman. She was wearing a plastic thing over her hair, sunglasses too. I immediately smiled and said, "Hey"—unable to move because my feet were off the ground. Then I got up and stood in the aisle—unable to stop smiling/laughing in a way that felt oh so bad.

ERIN AND HER FRIEND

1.

This girl Erin from where I used to work asked me if I'd escort her and her friend to a birthday party for another girl from work.

The party was in a bad neighborhood and they wanted me to come with them.

So I met them at the Wilson Red Line.

On the train, Erin sat next to me, and her friend sat in the seats in front of us, turned.

Erin punched my arm/neck and said, "What the fuck is wrong with you, smiley. Are you on drugs. You never smile."

I was smiling but I didn't know why.

"I'm just happy to be with you," I said.

Her friend stared at me the whole time.

Erin told me a couple days ago she wanted me to come out so her friend could, "...see you're hot and then you guys could have sex whenever you want, simple"—and she shrugged when saying it.

I looked out the window on the way to the party and tried not to make eye contact with anyone in the reflection, including myself.

2.

We went to a houseparty with basically only underage girls.

It was me, and then 47,000 high school girls, and like, 4 boys, all of them the brothers (?) of the birthday girl.

I was standing in a kitchen, with a crowd of teenaged girls around me drinking and yelling things.

One girl came up to me from behind and put her hands up and down my back and said, "Drink drink, we want to get you drunk. We want to take advantage of you."

She squeezed my back and said, "Oooooh" then all the girls started yelling again.

Everyone went to the same high school.

Oh.

This girl sitting on the countertop, she looked at me and said, "I want to go out to get cigarettes but I'm scared, will you come with me. Creepy dudes always yell at me when I'm there."

For some reason I started smiling and couldn't stop.

I said, "I don't know. Be brave,"

Erin said, "Uh uh bitch, he's here with us" grabbing my arm and putting her face against my shoulder.

The girl who wanted to take advantage of me kept rubbing my back.

I was being taken advantage of.

Sinking feet first into mud, with my hands up, me screaming, "She, took advantage of me, no" then the mud enters my mouth and nose and eyes.

This other girl tried to get me to drink from a bottle of tequila but then she dropped it when she was passing it and it broke all over the floor and everyone yelled at her and I helped her pick up the glass.

Then there was a crashing sound from a different room.

One of the boys pushed another boy out a first floor screen window and into some bushes and they started yelling at each other in the street.

I had to go out into the street to break up the "fight"—where one kid immediately took off his shirt and started quoting popular rap songs that expressed his anger and desire to fight.

Some guy I didn't recognize came out with a retractable

metal baton and for some reason immediately sided with me, saying, "Is it cool?" and I got everyone inside after someone else from across the street yelled, "We're going to call the fucking cops."

Back inside, I watched them all drink, and smoke marijuana.

I stood against the wall while teenaged girls stared at me and laughed and spoke spanish to each other behind red plastic cups.

Didn't know what I should be doing so I just stood there, sinking into mud, allowing the mud into my screaming mouth and eyes.

I thought—What if I just walk to the middle of the kitchen lay on the floor and refused to get up.

3.

People left slowly throughout the night.

Eventually everyone who was still there went into the living room and there was loud music and I sat down on a couch and the birthday girl came over.

She started asking me if I knew, if I knew, if I knew, if I knew she thought I was cute.

Then after I stared at her without blinking for a little bit she asked for a birthday hug.

She sat next to me and put her head on my shoulder and went to sleep within seconds.

Her friends all asked me to dance but I couldn't get up because the birthday girl was sleeping on me.

This other girl said, "Fuck that bitch, come on" and pulled me up.

The birthday girl woke up quickly, focused on us and smiled then went back to sleep with her head on the armrest.

I took turns dancing with the girls and I got really sweaty and they kept telling me I was a good dancer and every time

I'd yell, "No, you're a good dancer" to whoever said it.

4.

Later I walked a group of girls to the bus stop then returned to the party to escort other girls to other stops, as directed by Erin.

The whole time I walked a little away from the group as they moved down the block together in a weird formation, yelling shit at me every once in a while to remind me I was there and how was I doing man.

Had to stop at a gyro place so people could order food and I was waiting outside, enjoying the cool night when one of the girls opened the door and asked me to come in and sit with them so these other people would "shut the fuck up already."

I went in and sat with them while they ate.

One girl insisted on feeding me part of her pizza puff.

I had to both eat it and let her feed it to me.

5.

Last I took Erin and her friend home.

Blue Line to Red Line, all the way north to Rogers Park.

At the Red Line transfer, Erin and her friend sat on a bench hugging together to keep warm and I stood off to the side staring at a Chicago map posted by the garbage.

I looked at Chicago streets and imagined myself using thumbtacks to mark where my army will engage—myself pointing up into the air and nasally screaming, "Engage and destroy!" spitting all over the map.

This guy approached Erin and her friend.

He was wearing an oversized coat with small patches sewn all over—one for each team in the National Basketball Association —big jeans, woodtipped cigar behind his ear.

He put his foot up on the bench where the girls sat.

He motioned with his hands and licked his lips dramatically, and said, "Umma axyall som'." Then he licked his lips and folded his arms and said to Erin's friend, "Whassya name."

She said, "It's—"

And he held out his hand and said, "Nah, it's beautiful. It's unique. It's a living dream and an angel. It's my fantasy and my destiny."

"No, it's Val," she said.

He said, "Nah, it's powerful. Individual. It's essential."

Then he tried the same thing with Erin.

Erin was texting on her phone and didn't even look at him.

She put her hand up a little and said, "Nigga, just stop with the bullshit."

She pronounced "bullshit" like "boo shit."

That meant she was close to being violent.

I'd been punched hard by her moments after hearing her say "boo shit."

I stood there watching.

Erin's friend leaned forward and loudly said, "Yeah just leave us alone, we don't feel like being hit on right now ok, come on."

The guy clicked his teeth then backed up, assessing them both.

The first sounds of the train came through the tunnel and I went over to join the girls.

The guy took out the cigar from behind his ear then shook my hand and said, "Man, they yours? Good luck with boaf 'em. You lucky."

He walked away.

Erin and her friend and I got on the train, sat down in a mostly-empty car.

Erin said, "Nice fucking job, pussy. You're supposed to protect us."

I said, "He called you essential. I heard him say that."

Erin said, "Fiss" with her lips/teeth.

Her friend said, "No, he called me essential."

I said, "Which one of you was unique then."

Erin fixed her bra and took out a small plastic tube from her purse and applied something to her lips.

She said, "Shut the fuck up, pretty boy."

Then she smiled and touched my face and looked at me sweetly and said, "You are seriously, a pretty white boy."

Felt like I was in love with something but I didn't know what.

Maybe just all the negative space in front of me at all times.

6.

Back home, I saw Erin had sent me a message on my shitty prepaid phone.

The message was: "My friend said she wants to fuck you, bad."

I sent back: "Sounds good, Erin! Alright!" lying on the floor, waiting to go to sleep.

I imagined a double of myself falling through the ceiling and landing—in the "cannonball" position—on my face as I lay on the floor waiting to go to sleep.

PERSONALITY SHIELD

It happens now where someone tries to interact with me and we both just stand there while his/her personality bounces off my shield and hits the ground, instantly motionless.

ANOTHER THING ABOUT PERSONALITY

I've noticed sometimes when thinking about myself—like remembering a situation I was in or whatever—I don't visualize myself as how I actually look but instead as a pile of sticks.

ICE CREAM SANDWICH

I'm waiting out front my apartment building because I locked myself out.

On a bench nearby, a man and a woman talk about past drug use.

He did heroin and she did crack.

He's wearing a neon green fanny pack and a Bears sweatshirt and she's wearing all red—red shirt, red shiny stretch pants, and a red top hat.

He said, "Yeah I'm the kind of guy—it's like, I just love ice cream sandwiches so I'll just keep eating them know, if they're there, you know. It's like, that's how heroin was. Know, I like something I just keep doing it."

The woman laughs like, "Eh ah" and says, "Ice cream bars—shee yit."

"I lost all the feeling in my right hand, know," he said. "Stuff's bad."

She slaps both her thighs and turns her head a little sideways and says, "Zat all you did, fuckin herr-on."

He said, "No, I did stuff like uh, acid and pills too."

"Oooh," she says, cringing and leaning back a little. "Fuck allat weird shit, jo."

The man whistles two notes, staring forward.

He says, "Know, I just love ice cream sandwiches."

The way he's talking is like something is wrong with his throat or brain or other related part.

Like, I understand him, but the words are slightly different—like an accent from a country or region in which only he exists.

Then the woman in the shiny red top hat cites a few bible

verses—at times, angrily yelling them.

The man just sits there, staring forward through his tinted eyeglasses.

Green fanny pack.

Heroin.

Herr on.

The woman says, "Uh, yeah but uh, I's talkinna my susta and she was talking some URRitating shit. Mm!"

She starts seething a little.

Leans forward on the bench.

Begins pointing her finger downward in hard motions between her open legs.

She says, "I's like, 'I buss yo fucking head, talkinnat smart shit to me, bish.' To me! Fuck. BUSS, yo fucking head, bish."

The man just sits there—his hands folded over his lap, legs stretched out.

What is their relationship.

I want them to be married or getting married.

I want to be the only person at their wedding, where nothing is served except for ice cream sandwiches.

The woman uses the phrase 'buss yo head' for multiple other situations involving her sister and then she's actually on the ground, pointing and yelling.

Her yelling is scary.

She's yelling in a way that makes her voice sound demonic.

And the man just sits there looking forward.

I imagine him holding an ice cream sandwich against his face as the woman readies herself to punch him—saying, "buss yo fucking head" to herself over and over, covering her fist with the other hand—and then she swings her arm around like a windmill and punches the ice cream sandwich into his face.

And what would that do.

It would do a lot.

SAFE

On the Red Line train this guy gets into the car I'm in, right before the doors close. He stands there and says, "Safe! I made it!"—doing a baseball umpire motion for "Safe" holding an unpeeled banana in one hand and some mail in the other. Then he sits in the seat next to me, organizing the mail on his lap. He eats the banana and puts the peel in one of the opened envelopes. He is very calm and doesn't say anything else to anyone the whole time. Safe.

THINGS TO DO/SAY WHEN SOMEONE TRIES TO ENTER THE SINGLE-PERSON PUBLIC BATHROOM YOU'RE IN

1. You can relax, the door is locked. You don't have to say anything. Wait for the person to leave.
2. You can say, "Hey"—like, "Yeah, there's someone in here."
3. You can say, "Come on in."
4. You can say, "Yeah?" which does what #2 does but also means you're willing to answer questions (so be prepared to answer questions).
5. You can sit there quietly, hoping you remembered to lock the lock (because you just don't want to see people, not because it'd be embarrassing or whatever).
6. You can make a sound, like clearing your throat, to give the person a chance to realize there's someone else using the bathroom (this limits interaction).
7. You can pause, then in an unnaturally deep voice, say, "I've been waiting for you, sweetie."
8. You can sit there and quietly hope the person comes in and beheads you with a single uppercut to the chin.
9. You can sit there and quietly hope the place burns down with you trapped inside, and that a large assembly of city workers is required to remove your blackened corpse from its grip around the base of the toilet, screaming-face grafted to the porcelain and cooled.

NEIGHBORHOOD

Yesterday I saw a firetruck by this bank I used to go to and all the employees were out on the sidewalk.

I talked to one of the employees.

I said, "Is everyone ok."

She said, "Yeah, I think it's just something they have to check out real quick."

I said, "Because I used to bank here, and I wanted to make sure every thing's ok."

"Think everything's all right," she said, looking at her phone and scratching her elbow.

I said, "Ok good" and crossed the street.

On the next block, I saw a man sleeping facedown on a bench.

Hey, that's how I sleep—I thought, noticing I'd clapped my hands once and held them together.

Then I used the drawstring on my shorts for the first time.

It was nice.

A SQUIRREL

Last night I stretched in my girlfriend's room with the lights off. She was asleep and I stayed up to quietly stretch, staring out her window into the alley at the powerlines. A squirrel ran across the powerline five feet outside the window and stopped right across from me. I had the perfect view. The squirrel was carrying half a sandwich, holding it like a human with its short arms. Kept "nibbling" back and forth. Then while chewing, the squirrel would do this weird readjustment—like doing a juggling motion spinning the sandwich. And I tried not to laugh, because I didn't want to wake my girlfriend up because I wanted to enjoy it alone because it was meant for me because I just wanted to stretch quietly in the dark and watch a squirrel eat a sandwich.

MAKE A WISH

On the bus today, I stood up front by the driver with my back towards the direction we were moving, facing everyone else. And I made a wish for two giant hands to come from the sky—one with a dustpan and one with a broom. And I'd hold my thumbs up to signal, "Do your work."

DEMONS

Didn't notice I was doing this until I was doing it but, putting on a shirt today, I noticed I'd begun a "demon inspection"—holding out the arms of the shirt and checking underneath the collar. Then I didn't remember I'd done that until I was already doing it again with my boots.

PILE

The idea is to make yourself just a thin layer of dust that looks exactly like you, so when someone really tries to hurt you or get to know you s/he falls right through—already finished, both of you—and you end up on the ground in the same pile.

AIR CONDITIONER

I'm outside, kicking a rock around the dead-end that separates my block from the next. It's over a hundred degrees outside but still cooler outside my apartment than in it. I'm sweating. Feel sick. Across the street, a man exits an apartment building. He's wearing an oversized camouflage hunting coat and there's a huge bandaid on the side of his face. He leans against the front gate to the apartment building and smokes a cigarette. He starts doing this thing where he makes a face like someone is saying something to him, then he puts his head down, laughing. Over and over. I find myself quietly laughing along with him at one point then coming up with things the imaginary person is saying.

DUCT TAPE

I went to a hardware store to buy duct tape to fix my coat. Walking through the aisles, I smiled to myself and thought about saying, "Need some fucking duct tape here" in a tone of rising alarm, at random intervals, never making eye contact with anyone, and then I'm just screaming/shrieking on the floor (but actually I'm on the floor of my bathroom doing that, and I never went out for the duct tape).

ALCOHOLIC COUPLE

I was sitting on a bench out front of a grocery store, drinking some water I'd just bought.

There was a machine near me that allowed you to rent movies.

A homeless alcoholic couple came up to the machine and started scrolling through movies.

They both had on big winter hats, barely on the tops of their heads, sticking up really high.

The man said, "Oh, s'one has heroes. You like heroes right."

And the woman just pointed at the movie dispenser, chewing her toothless gums a little and squinting.

"Do y'wan me a tell you about a funny one then," the man said. "Or what. You like funny ones right."

The woman didn't say anything.

The man said, "This one has a war in it. Scary. Fighting. Hayyah!"

And he made some fighting motions with his hands.

I sat there listening to him describe each movie to her.

He'd read the description off the box in a loud monotone and then talk to her about it but she'd never answer.

"What about a love movie," he said. "Love is grand."

They scrolled through more movies.

I wanted to close my eyes and tell the man to imagine all the movies for me—just tell me what happens as I sit there the rest of the day.

"Tell me about heroes," I'd say, gently touching his arm, eyes closed. "Tell me about love."

THIS THING

I have this thing lately where I'll be out walking and I imagine myself taking out an assault rifle and shooting it at a car. And the bullets cross the windshield, spraying glass. And the person in the car gets out and opens fire on me with an assault rifle. Then more people come out—like from buildings or cars or wherever —and start shooting assault rifles at each other. No one dies or actually gets hurt though. It's just this loud, completely safe gun fight. Everyone wants everyone else to get hurt—and you feel the pain of what's happening—but no one actually gets hurt. And then the gunfire decreases, a few last shots. And we all put down the guns—which disappear on the ground—to continue doing whatever.

THIS THING [GRANDFATHER VERSION]

If I'm ever a grandfather, I want to have this thing where every time I see my grandkid(s) I always say, "Hey, now who's this little shithead?" and act like I don't know who it is for as long as it takes to upset the kid.

HOW I JUDGE PEOPLE NOW

I judge people by whether or not they like me. If they really like me, I almost can't like them. Or, I have to think more complexly in order to like them. But if they obviously don't like me, I feel immediate appreciation—an immediate bond—similar to if we both liked the same sports team or if we were both in the army together.

THE TREE STUMP ACROSS THE STREET

Every time I leave the apartment, I mistake the tree stump across the street for two people kissing/holding each other. I've forgotten every time that it's a tree stump. I'm disappointed every time it's a tree stump.

ABOUT THE AUTHOR

Sam Pinks's books include *Person*, *The No Hellos Diet*, *Hurt Others*, *Rontel*, *Witch Piss*, *The Garbage Times/ White Ibis*, and *The Ice Cream Man and Other Stories*. His writing has been published widely in print and on the Internet and translated into other languages. He currently lives in Michigan and sells paintings from instagram.com/sam_pink_art.

11:11 Press is an American independent literary publisher based in Minneapolis, MN. Founded in 2018, 11:11 publishes innovative literature of all forms and varieties. We believe in the freedom of artistic expression, the realization of creative potential, and the transcendental power of stories.

www.ingramcontent.com/pod-product-compliance
Lightning Source LLC
Chambersburg PA
CBHW030315100526
44592CB00010B/433